Photographs by
FRED J. MAROON

Text by
TOM WICKER

THE NIXON YEARS

1969 - 1974

WHITE HOUSE TO WATERGATE

ABBEVILLE PRESS

NEW YORK   LONDON

For my children, Marc,
Anne Hermine, Sophia, and
Paul, so they may better
understand this pivotal
period in our country's
political history. —F. J. M.

JACKET, FRONT
See page 52
JACKET, BACK
See page 64

PAGE 1
President Nixon signing legislation
into law in his San Clemente office.
January 13, 1971.

Even when on vacation at his
house in California, President
Nixon had official duties to
perform. A large number of his
staff traveled on Air Force One
with him; the executive branch of
government was wherever he was.

PAGES 2–3
At 8:30 in the morning, President
Nixon walks from the Residence
through the Rose Garden and directly
into the Oval Office on the right.
December 14, 1970.

A president's daily commute is
a short one; it involves walking
from the Residence part of the
White House to the Oval Office.
President Harry Truman used to
take long walks on the Mall and
elsewhere at dawn before starting
his day's work, and President
Clinton's jogging regularly made
the news, but outside of getting
to and from his office, Nixon was
not known to exercise in public.
When I shot this photograph,
I was glad to have any opportu-
nity, no matter how fleeting, to
capture him on film.

PAGE 7
President Nixon walking between
the columns to his office in the
West Wing. December 14, 1970.

On this brisk winter morning the
president waved hello to me,
disappeared between the columns,
and crossed the garden to a door
that led directly into his office.

Editor: Susan Costello
Production Editor: Kerrie Baldwin
Text Editor: Mary Christian
Art Director: Patricia Fabricant
Production Manager: Louise Kurtz

Design by Jim Wageman, Wigwag

Library of Congress Cataloging-in-
Publication Data

Maroon, Fred J.
   The Nixon Years, 1969-1974:
White House to Watergate/
photographs by Fred J. Maroon; text
by Tom Wicker.
   p. cm.
   Includes index.
   ISBN 0-7892-0610-2
   1. United States—Politics and government—1969-1974. 2. Nixon,
Richard M. (Milhous), 1913-1994.
3. Presidents—United States
Biography. I. Wicker, Tom. II. Title.
   E855.M37 1999
   973.924' 092—dc21
                              99-35265
                              CIP

First edition

10 9 8 7 6 5 4 3 2 1

ACKNOWLEDGMENTS

THIS BOOK'S CREATION SPANS A PERIOD of more than twenty-five years, and I am grateful and indebted to the many people who played roles during the various phases of the story. Louis Mercier, my business agent and mentor, was with me throughout the turbulent period that this book records, and provided patience and sage advice. The people at Leica Camera, and especially Walter Heun, introduced me to the new Leicaflex camera system in 1970, and that ensured the technical excellence of my equipment. There were many friends from those early years with whom it was good to renew acquaintance when I needed to enlist their help with some elusive identifications, especially Margita White, DeVan Shumway, Robert Odle, and Michael Putzel. The complicated story of Watergate has been eloquently tied together in this book by Tom Wicker, whose broad frame of reference has given balance and perspective to the events and players of the drama. Maureen Graney, my book agent, has been invaluable with her professionalism and generous with her insights. David Kennerly's persuasiveness and enthusiasm were a welcome influence on the final picture edit. I am extremely grateful to B. J. Cutler for reading my captions and giving me his counsel. Joshua Kaufman and Donald de Kieffer steered me through the legal shoals attached to works of this nature. The exhibition at the Smithsonian's National Museum of American History, whose opening coincided with this book's publication in July 1999, brought another dimension to the book's evolution and content. I shall always be indebted to Lonnie Bunch, Associate Director of Curatorial Affairs; Michelle Delaney, of the museum's Photographic History Collection; Larry Bird and Harry R. Rubenstein, curators in the Political History Division; Patrick Ladden, project manager; Hal Aber; Marcia Powell; and countless others who designed and organized the fine exhibition which is the counterpart of this book. Mary Panzer, Curator of Photography at the National Portrait Gallery, was enthusiastic from the outset, and invaluable when it came to making the final selection of photographs. Ashley Hansen, my able and tireless assistant, organized and prepared the work prints for the book and the exhibition in the summer of 1998. I cannot praise Murry Gelberg enough; his great vision and passion for all things artistic has been a constant inspiration to me. Richard Troiano, Zee Morin, and the darkroom technicians at Modernage in New York produced the superb final prints for the book and exhibition, and Pamela Chambers, of Imatek in Washington, made digital work prints that were better than I ever expected. I am especially grateful to Jim Wageman for his design, and to Robert Abrams, Susan Costello, and the editors at Abbeville Press for their consummate bookmaking skills, and for meticulously attending to all the demanding details that, in the end, determine the quality of a book. Last, but not least, my heartfelt thanks to my coauthor in all things, my wife Suzy, without whom this book would not exist. —F. J. M.

WHEN RICHARD MILHOUS NIXON BECAME PRESIDENT in 1969, I had been a freelance photographer in Washington, D.C. for seventeen years. At that time I was seldom in Washington, because I spent most of the time away working on exotic and far-flung assignments for a variety of national and international magazines. Photographing political figures and events, however, is a reality for any Washington-based photographer, and I did my share of it when I was in town.

Earlier, with the election of John F. Kennedy in 1960, Washington had undergone a sea change. It was no longer a sleepy southern town, having acquired a new glamour and status by virtue of the occupants of the White House. My first major feature on the White House was for *Look* magazine and was titled "Jacqueline Kennedy's New Look in the White House." It was followed by "Christmas in the White House." During the presidency of Lyndon B. Johnson, I began to contribute regularly to magazine articles about the White House; I had as many as one hundred pages of photographs published each year.

It was, therefore, with some surprise that I realized that these regular assignments had come to a sudden stop when Nixon became president. I was curious about why this happened, and when I mentioned the subject at story conferences with magazine editors, I was told that they were not interested in covering the new administration. Moreover, I discovered that the Nixon White House had no love affair with the press either, and they were very selective about press access to the White House. As a result, most Americans knew little about how the Nixon White House worked. The scarcity of photographic coverage of the White House presented a challenge to me. While the editors might not have been interested in the subject, I was very intrigued.

Several years earlier I had produced my first book on Washington, and I liked the luxury of space to tell a story that a book afforded. If any subject deserved to be a book rather than a magazine article, the White House did. I met with Herb Klein, the president's director of communications, and proposed doing a book on the Nixon administration—not just the president, but the workings of the entire White House staff. Allen Drury was to be the writer. The proposal was "staffed out," as they in the White House termed it, and, six months after my initial visit, the project was approved. The understanding was that neither photographs nor text were to be reviewed by the White House, and we were to receive full cooperation. For the most part, we did.

After the book was published in 1971, Attorney General John Mitchell was put in charge of the Committee to Re-elect the President (C.R.P. or CREEP, as it came to be known), with Jeb Stuart Magruder as his deputy. Magruder had been Herb Klein's deputy, and during a conversation with him early in 1972, he assured me that I could count on complete access should I wish to do any magazine story on the C.R.P. Armed with this commitment, I approached *LIFE* magazine and was guaranteed four pages for such a story. A week before the Watergate break-in, I telephoned Jeb Magruder to tell him of the *LIFE* assignment and to make arrangements to start photographing.

While I was working at the C.R.P. in the weeks immediately following the Watergate break-in, a discernible pattern developed. I would be allowed to photograph a meeting for ten or fifteen minutes and then I was always asked to leave. I can only imagine what key conversations must have taken place the minute I was safely out of the room. *LIFE* ran the four pages, selecting photographs that seemed important at the time. None of those photographs made the final cut for this book. Subsequent events have given other C.R.P. photographs —and individuals—far greater significance today.

In April 1973 a photo researcher at *Time* magazine requested a picture of John Dean. I was far too busy to spend much time searching for a head shot of a relatively unknown individual, but in the next few days the photo researcher called several more times, with ever increasing urgency. My agent in New York, Louis Mercier, and I realized that something important was breaking. In quick succession, one newspaper story after another appeared, culminating in the announcement of the Senate Watergate hearings. With my coverage of the major players in the Nixon White House and the C.R.P., I realized I had the beginning of an important historic photographic document, and I felt that I had no choice but to continue following the story as it unraveled. I canceled all other assignments and dedicated myself to covering the Senate Watergate hearings in their entirety in 1973. Each day I would drive from my house in Georgetown, allowing ample time to find a legal all-day parking spot on Capitol Hill. I then lugged two cases of cameras, lenses, and film several blocks before beginning my day's work in the Senate Caucus Room of the Russell Senate Office Building.

The impeachment hearings in the House of Representatives in the summer of 1974 became the next important phase in my ongoing documentation—then in its fourth year. Surprisingly, these hearings were sedate compared to the fireworks and conflicts that erupted between senators and witnesses during the lengthier and more highly charged hearings in the Senate. Also, as with the Senate, the House committee struck me as relatively nonpartisan. There were differences between the two parties, of course, but at the end of the day three articles of impeachment against President Nixon passed with both parties contributing to the results. Certainly there was less of the partisanship that characterized the Judiciary Committee in 1998 and 1999 during the impeachment proceedings against President Clinton.

In August 1974 my project ended where it began—in the White House. It was a far cry from the days in 1970 and 1971 when I had observed a staff in complete control of everything that happened there. During the week leading up to August 8, when President Nixon announced his resignation, uncertainty and apprehension prevailed. And the dramatic moment in the East Room the next day, when the president mustered up the strength and determination to say good-bye to his staff, cabinet, and friends, was like nothing any of us expected to experience.

One of the advantages of being a freelance photographer is that you are your own boss. It is often self-assigned work that best reflects the photographer and has the greatest long-term significance. Staff photographers may have the security of regular employment, but they seldom have the freedom to pursue their own muse. I am certain that, had I not enjoyed the independence I did, the Nixon document as seen here would not exist. Certainly there was little intimate coverage of the Nixon White House behind the scenes, and even if there had been, it is unlikely that the continuing chapters of the Watergate affair would have been assigned to the same photographer, with the same style and approach. It was because I was known to be neutral, unaffiliated with any political group or with any publication with a known political bias, that I was allowed access to the White House in the first place. And because I owned my own material, I could decide how it would eventually be used.

Early on I had decided that the material I collected would be under wraps until passions had cooled, and people could look at the photographs objectively and with historical perspective. After twenty-five years I realized that a nonpartisan view was never going to happen completely in my lifetime. Watergate and Nixon's resignation were such politically charged events that even today they arouse passions and debate. In 1997, aware that I wasn't getting younger, I decided to take my Nixon material out of storage and organize the story myself, rather than leaving it to strangers at some future time. From the 576 rolls I shot I made over a thousand work prints. For more than a year I edited the photographs, researched details, and refined the collection in order to arrive at the images in this book and in the exhibition held at the Smithsonian's National Museum of American History from July to December, 1999.

My four children were all under ten when their father thought that producing this archive was more important than having a steady income. I hope it gives them and others of their generation, as well as the generations to follow, a glimpse at the cast of characters who played important roles in this American drama—in what was, up to then, the greatest political tragedy our country has known.　　—FRED J. MAROON

INTRODUCTION

O N JANUARY 20, 1969, WHEN RICHARD MILHOUS NIXON WAS SWORN IN as the thirty-seventh president of the United States, he had come unimaginably far—a much greater distance than merely across the continent from Whittier, California. He had risen, of course, from early obscurity—as do most presidents. Unlike others, however, Nixon also had climbed out of the self-imposed ruins of a political career that had cast him from the heights of the vice presidency and a presidential candidacy of his own into near-disgrace and—perhaps worse—derision. Few politicians in history had risen so high or fallen so far, to rise again to the White House—the undisputed peak of American eminence. Few had been so despised or so admired by so many along the way.

He had been born in Whittier, near Los Angeles, in 1913 and grew up there, the son of Quaker parents—an argumentative, small-scale grocer and a mother often called by those who knew her (and by Nixon himself) "a saint." He was by all accounts a lonely, studious boy, working hard in his gruff father's neighborhood store, not much involved with girls, depressed by the deaths of two of his three brothers, the beneficiary of a splendid example of virtue—if not necessarily of effusive love—from saintly Hannah Nixon. Coming from a family too poor for him to accept a tuition scholarship to Yale, his first distinction was as a student leader and expert debater on the local campus of Whittier College.

There, young Richard deliberately avoided the Franklin Society, an organization for Whittier men of high social standing, and helped organize the rival group, the Orthogonians, mostly for those, like him, who were working their way through college. The Franklins wore tuxedos for their pictures in the college annual; the Orthogonians like Nixon wore open-collared white shirts. The Franklin-Orthogonian distinction seemed to remain a live contrast in Nixon's life—he always thought of himself as an Orthogonian and later on engaged in numerous confrontations with obvious Franklin types like Alger Hiss, Dean Acheson, Nelson Rockefeller, and John F. Kennedy.

Nixon was to excel as a law student on scholarship at Duke University, ranking third in a class of twenty-five. Unable in 1937 to find a position in the east, however, he was compelled to return to Whittier for his early law practice. This unpromising experience helped confirm his belief that he was an outsider, neither sophisticated nor brilliant, who could equal or prevail over more fortunate persons only by hard work and persistence—a recurrent theme in Nixon's life.

He spent World War II as a noncombatant naval officer on an island in the Pacific (military service being perhaps the first of many later violations of Hannah Nixon's Quaker faith). He was so skilled at playing poker that he could later return to civilian life with a small cash stake. But he was still in uniform in 1946 when Republican elders in Whittier—looking around for a presentable candidate against the supposedly powerful incumbent Democratic representative, Jerry Voorhis—offered the respectable young officer, Whittier College graduate, and former local lawyer the opportunity to seek a seat in Congress.

Nixon jumped at the opportunity, left the navy, and took to politics as if born to it, using his debating skills to particular advantage. Voorhis, moreover, was facing his first strong opponent and showed himself to be so inept a candidate that an apparent upset sent the neophyte Nixon to Washington with a reputation for being a giant killer. In victory, however, he had relentlessly pursued a tactic that was relatively new in 1946: implying that an opponent was "soft on" or dangerously ignorant about Communism, or even lacking in patriotism. A reputation for such jugular campaigning clung to him. In 1950, when he was elected to the U.S. Senate over a well-known Democratic congresswoman, Helen Gahagan Douglas, Nixon became notorious for such tactics. As a result, Mrs. Douglas pinned on him the label "Tricky Dick"—and it stuck for the rest of his long life.

By 1950 the new senator's pursuit of Alger Hiss already had made him a national political figure as an active and unapologetic anti-Communist. Hiss, who was accused of secret Communist activities by the former Communist courier Whittaker Chambers, was a former State Department official of high standing and a friend of Secretary of State Dean Acheson. In sessions of the House Un-American Activities Committee, Nixon assumed the lead in the Hiss investigation. Ultimately, Hiss was convicted of perjury (though not of spying, as Chambers had charged) and imprisoned. Nixon skillfully parlayed this heavily publicized Communist-hunting success into Republican leadership, election to the Senate, and—in 1952—his crowning triumph: selection as Dwight Eisenhower's vice presidential running mate. In an astonishingly brief public life—only six years—a high-flying career, as well as a haunting reputation, was launched.

In the 1952 campaign, Nixon survived a serious but temporary setback—a false charge that he had a secret political slush fund. In a celebrated television address that became known as the "Checkers" speech,[1] Nixon not only drew what was then the largest television audience ever assembled; he also refuted the charge and overcame the efforts of nervous Republicans to throw him off the national ticket. The episode may well have marked the beginning of Nixon's antipathy toward the press (the charge had originated in the New York *Post* and was trumpeted in many other newspapers); it also became a traumatic memory affecting Nixon through the many remaining years of his career.

For eight years as vice president, Nixon managed to picture himself as sitting at the right hand of Eisenhower, and actually was an unofficial acting president during "Ike's" two serious illnesses. That was deceptive; Nixon played an active *political* role but was never an influential member of the administration or an intimate of the president. Nevertheless, as a knowledgeable politician and party operator, he was able to consolidate his Republican leadership and take the 1960 presidential nomination with relative ease.

Few presidential candidates in history had been better known—for better *and* for worse—than was Richard M. Nixon in 1960. At age forty-seven, he appeared to have the future in his grasp. But in what by then were his fourteen eventful years in politics—covering the aftermath of World War II, the Korean War, the beginnings of the Cold War, and the world's mushrooming fear of nuclear destruction—that early reputation for "smear tactics" had remained a real and (somewhat unfairly) growing facet of his political persona. For that and other reasons—including his undoubted skill and success—"Tricky Dick" Nixon became the Republican that Democrats and liberals most loved to hate.

He proved in 1960, however, to be an uncertain presidential nominee, overmanaging his own campaign, wearing himself down physically, boosting his lesser-known opponent, John F. Kennedy, by appearing with Kennedy on national television in the first of the now-familiar presidential debates,[2] at one point appearing to spurn the Reverend Dr. Martin Luther King Jr., and allowing Eisenhower, the beloved father figure of the fifties, to be too little-used in the Republican campaign. In what turned out to be the closest, most disputed presidential election of modern times, Kennedy won by only about 118,000 votes out of more than 60 million cast—with the ironic result that Nixon's campaign gaffes appeared even more enormous, since each could have cost him and his party the victory and the presidency.

Nixon then made a cardinal political mistake: he yielded to Republican pleas and allowed himself to be the party's candidate for governor of California in 1962—in itself a comedown, after he had so nearly won the presidency. When he lost even a state governorship to the little-known Edmund G. ("Pat") Brown, and let himself appear in a maudlin (many thought drunken) "last press conference," Nixon was barely two years out of the vice presidency and national leadership. But two major defeats had given him a near-fatal loser's image; and national glee about the last press conference had demolished the idea of a young man inevitably headed for the top. It was widely believed he was finished—that in two years he had ruined what could have been a great political career.

In a hesitant, failed effort to win a second presidential nomination in 1964, Nixon appeared to have lost his political touch altogether. But in that same year he began a remarkable comeback with his farsighted support of Barry Goldwater, the conservative Republican candidate who was doomed to win only five states. Goldwater had little chance against Lyndon B. Johnson, in office less than a year after succeeding the murdered Kennedy, because American voters did not want a third president in less than twelve months. Republican leaders deserted Goldwater in droves, but Nixon stuck doggedly to his party. His hard campaigning in a lost cause was in such sharp contrast to others' abandonment of the Republican candidate that he regained much of his former stature as a party leader.

Nixon's comeback gained momentum in 1966 as he continued to impress both his party and the public with his tenacity and political intelligence. Gone—except from long Democratic memories—was the old Red-hunting, Red-baiting, self-styled "gut fighter," apparently replaced by an earnest new Nixon. Adroitly campaigning as a loyal, confident Republican only two years after the Goldwater debacle had all but shattered the party, the former vice president led a national Republican revival. It netted forty-seven new seats in the House and three in the Senate, landed the former movie star Ronald Reagan on the national scene as governor of California, and elected Nelson Rockefeller, a Nixon rival, to his third term as governor of New York.

It was thus a considerable understatement for Richard Nixon—with his much-derided "last press conference" four years in the past—to tell reporters that he "enjoyed listening to the 1966 election returns" because, as he later pointed out in *RN,* his memoir, "for the first time in ten years, I was identified with a smashing victory." Thus did Nixon—both loved and hated after twenty-two years, first at the top of the political world, then near its bottom—resurrect himself in 1968 as a leading presidential contender facing mostly feeble opposition from Rockefeller, Reagan, and Governor George Romney of Michigan.

On the Democratic side, chaos seemed to reign in 1968, owing much to the surging unpopularity of "Johnson's war" in Vietnam, but just as much to the close identification of the president and his party with a black community emerging from the long years of segregation more bumptiously than most white Americans had expected, or wanted. In March, Senator Eugene McCarthy of Minnesota, an almost unknown antiwar candidate, nearly upset Johnson in the New Hampshire primary. Then an even more formidable antiwar figure, Robert Kennedy, announced his candidacy—whereupon Johnson startled the nation by declaring that he would neither seek nor accept renomination by the Democrats. These shocks were followed in tragic succession by the assassinations of Martin Luther King, further stirring racial turmoil, and of Robert Kennedy, just hours after he had defeated McCarthy in the California primary in June 1968.

Nixon, meanwhile, had proceeded, almost as a king to his coronation, to his second Republican presidential nomination. In the general election of 1968, he was to contest the Democratic candidate, Vice President Hubert H. Humphrey, who was regarded by many as little more than Lyndon Johnson's lackey, and Governor George Wallace of Alabama, who waged a spirited third-party race blatantly exploiting racial fears. In another hard-fought campaign Nixon avoided the personal and political mistakes of 1960; he supported the war in Vietnam but criticized its conduct, and promised both to end (though not to abandon) it and "win the peace." Importantly, he eschewed the racist extremes of the Wallace campaign, but his so-called "southern strategy" more subtly and effectively allowed southerners and other alarmed whites to assume that he would be less vigorous than Johnson had been in enforcing racial integration.

Finally, therefore, in January 1969, after nearly a quarter-century of unflagging effort and after an election almost as close as that of 1960, Richard M. Nixon—still loved and hated, still nursing the grievances of a political lifetime—entered the White House to face a daunting world.

A powerful Democratic Congress—united, if on anything, by its mistrust of "Tricky Dick" Nixon—seemed a fixture on Capitol Hill. The war in Vietnam clearly was not being won, and many believed it lost; questions about its bloodshed, costs and legitimacy bitterly divided the American public. School desegregation and other divisive racial matters seemed intractable. Crime, suddenly a national rather than a local issue, had been rising spectacularly. The seemingly endless Cold War continued both to force extravagant defense expenditures and to pose the specter of nuclear catastrophe.

The fulfillment of Nixon's presidential ambition—a vindication so long in coming, so difficult in the making—may also have caused him to forget momentarily what in a less exuberant period he had confided to the journalist Earl Mazo: "The one sure thing in politics is that what goes up comes down, and what goes down often comes up."

In the years to come, Nixon was to be forcibly reminded of this hard-earned wisdom—not just by his political, but by his personal trials. For one thing, he had a high sense of presidential powers (perhaps because he had been barred from them for so long), and insisted on the honor and respect he believed was due him. Those around him naturally acquiesced in their own self-interest, but his attitude betrayed—and was reinforced by—Orthogonian personal insecurities and self-doubt. Secretive by nature, convinced that in his chosen field of expertise—foreign affairs—secrecy was vital to success (an outlook shared and spurred by Henry Kissinger, his national security adviser), Nixon was also an embittered man, conscious of his grudges, persuaded by experience that most people did not like him and that the press was his implacable enemy.

"We've got the reputation of . . . building a wall around the President," one of his close assistants, John Ehrlichman, said of himself and H. R. ("Bob") Haldeman, the chief of staff. "The fact is that he was down under the desk saying 'I don't want to see those fellows,' and we were trying to pull him out."

On the other side of the coin, the reclusive Nixon is the only president in memory who could sit alone in a "hideaway" office in the Executive Office Building and outline his own—often highly effective—speeches on a yellow legal pad. But combined with what Ehrlichman considered a "narrow range of interests," his penchant for solitude also led Nixon to allow many domestic matters to be handled by his cabinet officers and other aides. Most fatefully, he left his major political efforts in 1972 to the Committee to Re-elect the President.

Despite his years in politics and high office, Nixon also could be strangely ignorant of political realities. After their first meeting, Daniel Patrick Moynihan was startled by "the things that Nixon said he didn't know." Nixon later insisted that he had a right to "appoint" Supreme Court justices, though the Constitution gives a president only the lesser power to "nominate" and the Senate the right to confirm or reject a nominee. He suggested to David Frost that the approval of a president could make legal what ordinarily would have been an unlawful act. He frequently confused (or deliberately linked) his own political interests with "the best interests" of the nation, and he had no doubt of his ability to gull the press and the public about either—and he had little hesitation in doing so.

Thus, even as he had achieved his highest ambition, as men rose to their feet and the band played "Hail to the Chief" when he entered a room, Richard Nixon could not be entirely comfortable or feel entirely safe, even in the White House. He still felt himself an Orthogonian outsider. Encouraged by a circle of sycophants (as all presidents tend to be), Nixon seemed to withdraw further into himself and make the Oval Office into a fortress of isolation and secrecy. The enemies he sensed all about were mostly imaginary. But, like a hypochondriac who actually falls ill, he was genuinely disliked, even hated by powerful forces he did not need to imagine.

Echoing George Wallace, if in more moderate words, Nixon had promised in the 1968 campaign to bring "law and order"—a phrase in those years so familiar that it often seemed a single word: "law'norder"—to a nation more fearful every day of crime in the streets, race riots in the cities, and Vietnam protests on the campus. On January 20, 1969, as he rolled along Pennsylvania Avenue to his inauguration in an armored limousine (fancifully described by "gonzo journalist" Hunter S. Thompson as a "huge, hollowed-out cannonball on wheels"), sticks, stones, beer cans, and an occasional firecracker were thrown from a crowd chanting "Ho, Ho, Ho Chi Minh, the N.L.F. is going to win."[3]

Nixon, power his at last, was having none of that—not on his watch. Standby troops dispersed the crowd. Later that day, the new president sent Ehrlichman a copy of a Washington *Evening Star* editorial lamenting that no demonstrator had been arrested, with a note demanding, "Why not? I think an opportunity was missed when people would have suggested taking action." In a separate note, Nixon added that "it is of the highest priority to do something meaningful on . . . crime."

The Nixon administration was off to a portentous start. Plenty of "meaningful" action—not all of it authorized from the top—soon would be taken by the new men in Washington, all anxious for the approval of their belligerent leader. Such action would lead to a taped-over lock in the Watergate Office Building, and ultimately to the first resignation of a president in American history.

1. This was named for Nixon's reference in the address to his family's dog, Checkers, which had been a gift to his two daughters.
2. For which, finally, a new record television audience exceeded that for the "Checkers" speech in 1952.
3. Ho Chi Minh was the North Vietnamese leader, and the National Liberation Front was the spearhead of the revolutionary fighting in South Vietnam.

THE FIRST TERM

PAGES 16–17
The limousine of
Richard Milhous
Nixon, thirty-
seventh president
of the United States,
leading the motor-
cade down Pennsyl-
vania Avenue under
heavy security dur-
ing his inaugura-
tion. January 20, 1969.

*All inaugural
parades demand
a high level of
security, but this
one had more than
any I had ever
seen. Shoulder-to-
shoulder, soldiers
lined the entire
route in front of
the spectators, and
the Secret Service
surrounded the
motorcade so
completely that
bystanders were
lucky to get even
a brief glimpse of
the new president.*

MERICANS WHO ARE FORTY-THREE YEARS OLD OR YOUNGER TODAY—
a lot of Americans—would have been too young to vote for or
against Richard Nixon for president, even in 1968 or 1972. Most
probably remember little except one thing about him: that he was the only
president ever to resign under threat of being impeached by the House of
Representatives. And they may know almost nothing, save perhaps of his
stubborn continuation of the war in Vietnam, about his presidency from
1969 until 1974.

That's understandable. The Watergate scandal and Nixon's forced
departure from office are unique in American history, monumental facts that
stand like an impenetrable wall between the first Nixon term and later recognition of its record. Everyone knows about his resignation—if only from his
obituary in 1994—and something about what caused it; it's too bad, however, that so few can see past that thick wall to the years when the Nixon
administration accomplished much that was admirable then, and still would
be remarkable in today's far different political atmosphere.

Senator Daniel Patrick Moynihan of New York, a Democrat who risked
his party's disapproval to serve as a domestic advisor in the first Nixon
administration, remarked almost two decades later that he was proud to have
served in what he still considered "the most progressive" administration of
the postwar era. That judgment will come as a surprise to younger Americans
if they think of Nixon only as a sort of conservative precursor of Ronald
Reagan, and a trampler of the Constitution at that.

Conservative he was, for his time, but by no means in the political
sense that later described Reagan or such hard-right congressional Republicans as Dick Armey of Texas and Jesse Helms of North Carolina. Richard
Nixon's political life had commenced in 1946, when the New Deal and Harry
Truman's Fair Deal represented the reigning spirit of the times. His career
unfolded almost entirely within that ethos, even as the old liberalism slowly
began to fade. Dwight Eisenhower's two terms in the White House and
Nixon's uncomfortable eight years in the vice presidency were notable for
modern, not old guard, Republicanism. In fact, Nixon had been picked as
Ike's running mate, and could win the party's presidential nomination in
1960, not least because he had carefully maintained links to both its wings—
to "modern" Republicans like Thomas E. Dewey of New York and to old
guardians like Styles Bridges of New Hampshire.

Nixon's party and national victories in 1968 demonstrated that a moderate approach—"centrist," he called it—still was politically profitable even in

that late year; and it is far more logical to see Barry Goldwater and George Wallace in their 1964 and 1968 campaigns as having paved the way for Ronald Reagan and the conservative revolution than to cast Richard Nixon in that role. Moynihan's judgment will be disputed by many Democrats and liberals—particularly by partisans of Harry Truman and John F. Kennedy—but the record provides solid evidence that the Nixon administration, if not the "most" progressive of the postwar era, was far from typically "conservative."

The Environmental Protection Agency, for one good example, was established in the first Nixon term and at the president's behest; indeed Russell Train, the chairman of a council of environmental advisers in the first Nixon administration, makes the plausible claim that Nixon did more for the environment than any other president. The National Environmental Policy Act, a congressional initiative, was pushed through by Nixon, who also gave important support to the Clean Air Act of 1970 and much other environmental legislation. He canceled the environmentally damaging Cross-Florida Barge Canal; created numerous national parks; and, in 1970, with another huge television audience tuned in, made protection of the environment the central theme of his State of the Union message.

These events were not untypical of the Nixon administration, because they happened despite the fact that Richard Nixon personally was by no means an environmentalist. He vetoed a Clean Water Act in 1972 and once told a speech writer, "In a flat choice between smoke and jobs, we're for jobs." But as a politician he recognized a fruitful line of action ("there's mileage in it," he would say of such issues), particularly after the enthusiastic public response to the first Earth Day in 1970. Many a president has thus acted politically rather than from pure or idealistic motives—but often to a useful purpose and better results.

Though Nixon doubted black Americans could be converted en masse to the Republican party, he also pushed a program (with only limited success) to give black entrepreneurs a "piece of the action" in a bustling American economy. During his administration, the volunteer army was approved, and under the prodding of Secretary of Labor George Shultz, the Nixon administration adopted the "Philadelphia Plan"—an early affirmative-action program that required labor unions working on federally financed projects in that city to open their (formerly lily-white) ranks to blacks.

Nor was conservative Richard Nixon hand-in-glove with big business in the traditional Republican manner. Indelibly aware that recession had damaged his 1960 presidential campaign, and that President Eisenhower had nevertheless refused to "prime the pump," Nixon was keen to avoid unemployment in his own administration. He even proclaimed himself a Keynesian in an interview with the television reporter Howard K. Smith and adopted a "jawboning" policy in an attempt to influence private wage-and-price decisions. Approving a balanced budget for 1970—the last the nation has had—he courted Republican wrath by continuing the Vietnam-forced income tax surcharge passed at Lyndon Johnson's urging in 1968.

For fiscal 1972, again at the instigation of George Shultz (who later became secretary of the Treasury), Nixon announced a revolutionary "full-employment budget"—one based on the premise that revenues would come in at the same rate as if the economy were at full employment, which it decidedly was not. The resulting deficit was deliberately calculated to stimulate the economy.

In view of these economic unorthodoxies, perhaps it's not surprising—though it's still little-credited—that Richard Nixon became the first peacetime president in history to impose wage and price controls on the economy, while at the same time he took the even more radical step, in the business view, of suspending the convertibility of the dollar into gold. More conventionally expressed, he took the nation off the gold standard, and later abandoned dollar convertibility altogether.

In foreign affairs, the area in which Nixon took the greatest interest and made the largest claims, he and Henry Kissinger negotiated and the president signed the first arms control treaty with the Soviet Union (on terms mostly developed, but not pursued, in the late stages of the Johnson administration). The first Cold-War détente followed (briefly), and Nixon later took a hitherto unthinkable step that resulted in what was unquestionably the major achievement of his presidency—the so-called "opening to China." As critics often said, the old Nixon surely would have denounced the new Nixon for this diplomatic heresy that led to the two nations' mutual recognition. But much evidence suggests that he had been contemplating, but not advocating, rapprochement with China at least since the Sino-Soviet split in the early 1960s. Indirection was often Richard Nixon's crafty way.

Domestically, Nixon's most trying problem was school desegregation—owing to his support in the South and his campaign strategy of appearing less willing to enforce racial integration than Johnson had been. Although the Supreme Court's *Brown v. Board of Education* decision had been in 1954, as late as the fall of 1968 only 18.4 percent of 3.2 million black elementary and secondary school pupils in the South were enrolled in schools that were 50 percent or more white. Nearly 79 percent were *still* in schools 80 percent or more black.

By 1970, federal court orders left Nixon no choice but to move ahead with desegregation, despite his campaign attitude. But he had established good relations with southern leaders and had a close bond of trust with many of them—for instance, Senator Strom Thurmond of South Carolina—and made strong, if failing, efforts to name to the Supreme Court two southerners—Clement Haynsworth and Harold Carswell. Ironically, their successive defeats by a Democratic Senate improved the Republican Nixon's political standing in the South and strengthened his hand in pushing school desegregation, under court pressures he could not ignore.

The result was remarkable: the percentage of blacks in mostly white schools rose to 38.1 percent, while the percentage in heavily black schools dropped to 41.7. That remains the biggest single-year increase in southern school desegregation. It is not too much to say that, as much as any president before or since, Richard Nixon presided over the end of dual school systems in the South.

President Nixon at his desk in the Oval Office. February 10, 1971.

"He comes in in the morning and sits down in that chair, and that's where he stays all during his working day," remarked one presidential aide. It was very quiet in the president's office; the only interruption was the sound of rustling paper as he finished reading each page. I knew that anything that had made it this far for his consideration had to be important, as indicated by his solemn concentration. I used a range-finder Leica M camera so the sound of the shutter clicking would not be so distracting as to get me thrown out of the office.

President Nixon at a
cabinet meeting in the
Cabinet Room prior to
his announcement of a
cease-fire in Vietnam.
October 7, 1970.

In Courage and Hesitation, *Allen Drury
quoted sources who maintained that the
president did not use his cabinet enough,
but he had set up a powerful staff in the
White House that did much of what the
cabinet traditionally did.*

In the Oval Office
(left to right):
Henry Kissinger,
Imelda Marcos,
and President and
Mrs. Nixon have
a light moment
during conversation.
September 22, 1970.

*President Nixon entertained foreign guests
regularly. The visit of Imelda Marcos,
whose husband was president of the
Philippines, provided a rare opportunity
for me to photograph Mrs. Nixon in the
Oval Office, too. It was the first of several
occasions where I was able to capture
the warmth and affection between the
president and his wife.*

Nixon had a hideaway office in the Executive Office Building, next door to the White House, and I was taken there to photograph him as he prepared for a television address. He scarcely moved from his seat the entire time I was there. I kept hoping he might answer the telephone or walk around the room, so I could get some variety, but it didn't happen. Later, in the Press Room, I overheard some White House correspondents commenting on how formal the president always was. One said, "I bet he takes a shower in that suit!" Another added, "If a photographer ever photographed him with his feet up, it would be worth a million dollars."

President Nixon working on a television speech in his office in the Executive Office Building. October 7, 1970.

British Prime Minister Edward Heath arriving on the South Lawn of the White House for a state visit. December 17, 1970.

The arrival of a chief of state is always an occasion of pomp and ceremony, replete with military bands, national anthems, and speeches. A large crowd of invited guests is on hand, including diplomats, cabinet members, congressmen, White House aides, personal friends, and the press. On this occasion the White House police, seen saluting in the foreground, were sporting their new white uniforms. President Nixon had decided that the uniforms of the White House police were not as grand as some he had seen in other countries, and had ordered that a much flashier version be designed. It was rumored that helmets had been produced to augment the already highly questionable effect, but the outcry over the initial unveiling was such that the whole idea was quickly scuttled.

Israeli Prime Minister Golda Meir and President Nixon during a "photo op" in the Oval Office. Itzhak Rabin sits on the couch to Mrs. Meir's right. September 18, 1970.

Because American presidents have long had high on their agendas the problems in the Middle East, the heads of state from that region are always accorded special attention. On this occasion, after the press had left, the president was reported to have remarked, "You know, Madam Prime Minister, you and I have one thing in common: our key foreign affairs advisers are both Jews." To which Mrs. Meir replied, "Yes, Mr. President, but mine speaks English!"—a reference to her impeccably British-accented foreign affairs minister, Abba Eban.

OPPOSITE
President Nixon and Soviet Foreign Minister Andrei Gromyko in conversation en route to the White House from the Executive Office Building. October 22, 1970.

When Andrei Gromyko came to Washington, Nixon met with him in his private office in the Executive Office Building. The two men walked back together to the West Wing and continued to confer before holding a press conference. It was shortly after this meeting that construction of a submarine base by the Soviets in Cuba ceased completely.

Murray Chotiner
(left) and Charles
W. Colson, special
counsel to the
president, at a
high-level political
meeting held in the
Executive Office
Building in the last
month before the
1970 election.
October 7, 1970.

*Chuck Colson had been cordial to me
when I first photographed him, as here,
at a political meeting. In* Courage and
Hesitation, *Allen Drury quoted an
anonymous congressman as saying that
Colson and Murray Chotiner were Nixon's
"hatchetmen." That certainly wasn't
evident to me as I waited for the right
expression and gesture.*

It was at this meeting that I first became aware of the hierarchy of command and the delegation of authority as it worked within the White House. Prior to this meeting, I had photographed Ken Cole in his office, and repeatedly I heard him say to those around him or on the telephone, "I'll take this up with John," or "I don't think I can show John that." Now here was John! Ehrlichman fielded papers from Cole and Tod Hullin, tossed out a terse remark, or asked for a further briefing.

He carefully studied every paper handed to him. He either said "yes" or "no," or "I'll take it up with the president." It was at this time that a report on obscenity was being bandied about by the press. Ehrlichman asked Cole whether they had a copy, and was told that he had not been successful in getting one. Ehrlichman shot back with a twinkle in his eye: "What's wrong? Doesn't the White House have any clout? Get a copy of that report."

Nightly meeting in John D. Ehrlichman's office brings together Ehrlichman (right), assistant to the president for domestic affairs; Kenneth R. Cole Jr. (far left), deputy assistant to the president for domestic affairs; and staff assistant Tod R. Hullin. October 22, 1970.

H. R. Haldeman
in his office in
the White House.
November 24, 1970.

A man's office tells a lot about him. His importance in the White House determined his office's location and size, but the occupant had a lot to say about its decor. H. R. ("Bob") Haldeman, chief executive officer of the White House, had a spacious office that was decorated in a Williamsburg style. It was a no-nonsense office, efficiently designed for the high-powered role of its occupant and the meetings that occurred there. Haldeman ran a tight ship.

He held the keys to the gate of the "Berlin Wall" around the president and was described by Newsweek magazine as "probably the most powerful man in the country next to the president." It was after this session with him that he asked how my project was going. I told him I was getting some things but not as much high-level coverage, including of the president, as I would like. Shortly after that my access improved, especially to the Oval Office.

Haldeman's office was the location of regular 8.00 A.M. meetings prior to Haldeman's morning appointment with the president. Those attending were the president's closest advisers; it was one of the highest level staff meetings to which I was invited. This, and the 7:00 A.M. meeting chaired by John Ehrlichman

and George Shultz, introduced me to the sequence of events that occurs each morning before the president's official day begins. The meeting had been under way about fifteen minutes when Ron Ziegler arrived, and from the expression on his face I could see he was not pleased to see me.

A high-level staff meeting in the office of H. R. Haldeman, 8:00 A.M. Left to right: John Ehrlichman, George Shultz, Ronald Ziegler, the president's press secretary, Bryce Harlow, Donald Rumsfeld, Haldeman, Robert Finch (with back to camera, at right). November 25, 1970.

In the last week of
the 1970 campaign,
Vice President Spiro
Agnew relaxes in
the presidential suite
of the Holiday Inn,
Wichita, Kansas.
October 29, 1970.

*A midterm stump for local candidates
in 1970 brought Spiro Agnew to Wichita,
Kansas. The campaign trail seemed to be
the place the vice president was at his most
effective. I saw him speak to all sorts of
people—from student hecklers who would*

*force him to deviate from his text to
staunch supporters who would greet him
with roars of adulation. But I wanted to
capture him in a private moment, because
away from the public he was always a
soft-spoken person.*

OPPOSITE, TOP
Patrick Buchanan,
assistant to the
president, with Vice
President Agnew
and the press during
a stopover on the
1970 campaign trail.
October 30, 1970.

*Vice President Agnew had his own unique
style and usually spoke more forthrightly
than the president himself. The press had
a field day with some of Agnew's character-
izations. "Nattering nabobs of negativism"
drew howls of ridicule, and "effete snobs,"
originally directed at a small group of
activists who were encouraging student
riots, was quickly expanded by the press
to refer to all American youth.*

OPPOSITE, BOTTOM
Vice President Agnew
with his wife (center),
and staff, viewing
the 1970 election
returns in his hotel
suite in November
1970. At right: Patrick
Buchanan, assistant
to the president.
November 3, 1970.

*Pay-off time for
all politicians
and campaign
workers is when
the election returns
come in. Tension
mounts as sober
reality replaces
sometimes un-
founded optimism.*

ABOVE
In a White House corridor (left to right): George Shultz, director of the Office of Management and Budget; Caspar Weinberger; John C. Whittaker, deputy assistant to the president for domestic affairs; and John Ehrlichman. November 25, 1970.

This photograph of men arriving for a meeting has a more candid quality than the meeting itself. For the men, it was a chance to discuss things privately. As the major players became familiar with me, they acted naturally around me and my camera.

ABOVE, RIGHT
Ron Ziegler, the president's press secretary, and Attorney General John Mitchell, waiting to enter the Oval Office. April 20, 1971.

For these men, entering the Oval Office was an everyday affair; for most others it was high anxiety time. By the time I made this photograph I had had a number of opportunities to be with the president, but I could always feel the adrenaline pumping in anticipation until I actually started shooting.

OPPOSITE
President Nixon in the Oval Office with Representative Gerald R. Ford. December 14, 1970.

President Nixon often met with members of Congress. This photograph shows the president's cordial relationship with Gerald Ford years before the Watergate crisis dramatically changed their respective roles.

Principal members of President Nixon's executive staff attending the daily 7 A.M. meeting in the Roosevelt Room of the West Wing. Chaired by presidential advisers John Ehrlichman and George Shultz. December 15, 1970.

I was unaware that the White House started functioning at this hour. It seemed that I was being asked to arrive earlier and earlier. I even attended this 7.00 A.M. meeting. None of the White House guards had

ever seen a photographer show up for these early meetings, and they did a lot of double-checking before they let me pass. Finally, I would get the okay and would be taken to the meeting, which would be

already under way. I figured that to be there, these men had to get up by 6 A.M. or earlier, and since they had often not finished until late the night before, it certainly couldn't have left them much time for their families. There was always a strong sense of concern in these meetings. The problems under discussion were huge, demanding the utmost concentration and discipline. And the camera picked that up.

Diane Sawyer (left), and Mary Alice Passman (right) in Ron Ziegler's reception area off the Press Room. December 15, 1970.

I spent a lot of time in the White House sitting in the Press Room waiting for Ron Ziegler or someone else to notify me of an opportunity to photograph Nixon. I took this picture simply for the record, never dreaming that the young woman on the left would become familiar to more Americans than most of the major players in the White House.

Speech writer William Safire, special assistant to the president, during a Saturday morning "Plans Committee" meeting. December 19, 1970.

At this meeting Safire and the "Plans Committee" were discussing how to correct an inadvertent slight: the president had not been photographed with a small black poster girl, and the omission, of which he was unaware, caused resentment in the African-American community, especially since he was later photographed with a little white poster boy. By the time the president heard about it the media had gone into full cry, and Nixon's aides were faced with correcting an avoidable embarrassment.

The "Plans Commit-
tee" meeting held
every Saturday
morning in Herb
Klein's office in
the Executive Office
Building. Left to
right: Herb Klein,
director of commun-
ications for the
executive branch;
Leonard (Lyn)
Nofziger, director
of communications
for the Republican
National Committee;
Dwight Chapin,
deputy assistant to
the president; and
Jeb Stuart Magruder,
deputy director
of White House
Communications.
December 19, 1970.

The "Plans Committee," also known as
the "image factory," met to discuss matters
affecting the president's public image. This
was complicated by Nixon's belief that the
vast majority of the press corps was deter-
mined to present his administration in the
harshest possible light. I am sure my pres-
ence in the White House was approved at
just such a meeting. I had been told that
there were two dissenting votes on that
occasion; during the course of my work in
the White House, I often wondered who
might have cast them.

President Nixon at
the University of
Nebraska. January
14, 1971.

*On the way back to
Washington from
San Clemente the
president spoke at
the University of
Nebraska, where
he was warmly
greeted. Up to this
point, I had trav-
eled with him on
Air Force One, but
when I reported
back to the plane
to continue the
trip to Washington,
I was directed to
the regular press
plane. I thought
it was too good to
last. When we got
back to Washing-
ton, Ron Ziegler,
the president's
press secretary,
reprimanded me
for talking to the
president after
photographing him
in San Clemente
and wanted to
know what we
had talked about.*

OPPOSITE
President Nixon
and John Connally
face the press to
announce Connally's
appointment as
secretary of the
Treasury, replacing
David Kennedy.
December 14, 1970.

*This is one of the
few "news" photo-
graphs I took in
the White House;
President Nixon
was introducing
the press to the
man he nominated
as secretary of the
Treasury. At the
time I thought that
John Connally of
Texas looked "pres-
idential." Later I
watched him rise
in stature and
importance, and
for a while this
picture appeared
quite prophetic.*

Attorney General
Mitchell hosts
a luncheon in
his dining room
at the Department
of Justice.
October 2, 1970.

*During this luncheon Attorney General Mitchell
was handed a note that visibly upset him. "Who
gave her a visa?" he demanded. He was told that
the State Department had issued a visa to Mrs.
Nguyen Cao Ky, the wife of the vice president of
South Vietnam, so she could attend a mass rally
on the Mall in Washington. Mrs. Ky's presence at
the rally could only make a bad political situation
worse for the administration. "Where is she now?"
Mitchell asked. "Over the Atlantic," came the reply.
"Can we have the plane land in Boston?" "What
reason can we give?" "I don't know—quarantine,
epidemic, anything, I don't care!" The matter was
still unresolved when I left, but the next morning
I heard on the radio that a commercial flight
with Mrs. Ky on board had developed engine
trouble and had turned back for an emergency
landing, making it impossible for her
to attend the rally!*

OPPOSITE
President Nixon at
a congressional
luncheon in the
United States Capitol.
September 15, 1970.

*President Nixon
cultivated good rela-
tions with members
of Congress by meet-
ing with them on
their turf and invit-
ing them to meet on
his. He himself had
served in both the
House and the Sen-
ate before becoming
Eisenhower's vice
president in 1952.*

A group of senators meets with President Nixon, back to camera, and members of his administration in the Oval Office. On his couch at left are Elliot Richardson, secretary of Health, Education, and Welfare, and Senator Wallace Bennett. Behind, from the left, are John Ehrlichman, Senator Daniel Patrick Moynihan, Senator Hugh Scott, Senator Russell Long, Ron Ziegler (standing), and Senator Mike Mansfield.
December 30, 1970.

President Nixon succeeded in maintaining the allegiance of conservatives even as he pursued a centrist, almost liberal, domestic policy.

George Shultz, back to camera, talks with John Ehrlichman in the Cabinet Room prior to a cabinet meeting. To the left is former governor George Romney talking with General William Westmoreland, and on the far right, Caspar Weinberger, with Arnold Webber. October 7, 1970.

To be in the Cabinet Room prior to the president's arrival meant having an opportunity to capture key members of the administration interacting with each other. I was able to maneuver among them, composing and photographing targets of opportunity without anyone paying any attention to me.

Al Haig and Henry Kissinger were the key members of the National Security Council. The Council's Situation Room, or, as I heard it called, the "War Room," looked pretty sanitized when I photographed it. There were some maps of Vietnam on the wall, but little else.

Brigadier General Alexander M. Haig (at left), deputy assistant to the president for national affairs, talks to Commander Jonathan T. Howe, National Security Council staff, in the basement of the West Wing of the White House. January 9, 1971.

Henry Kissinger, in flight jacket, chats with members of the press pool on *Air Force One*. Left to right: Gerrold L. Schecter, *Time* magazine; Robert Pierpont, CBS; and Helen Thomas, UPI. January 14, 1971.

The majority of the press corps traveled in a separate plane when President Nixon traveled outside of Washington but to be selected for the press pool on Air Force One *was highly desirable. The long trips often provided pool reporters with unusual opportunities to gather information or stories from officials on the plane. Members of the press who wrote unfavorable stories about the White House were sometimes denied access to* Air Force One.

President and Mrs. Nixon on board the presidential helicopter en route from San Clemente to El Toro Marine Base, where he would board *Air Force One*. January 14, 1971.

Mrs. Nixon sat directly across from the president, but they never spoke. Occasionally, lost in his own thoughts, he would gaze out the window in meditation.

Tricia Nixon; Rose Mary Woods, the president's personal secretary; Commander Charles R. Larson; and President Nixon on board the presidential helicopter. January 14, 1971.

It was interesting how detached Nixon was from everyone else on the helicopter. The others spoke or laughed together, but the president talked to no one except briefly to Commander Larson, who gave him a folder to work on.

President Nixon
is lost in thought
while working in
the presidential
helicopter.
January 14, 1971.

*After I had completed a photo session
with the president in San Clemente, he
asked if I was satisfied with the way my
book project was going. Of course, I stated
the obvious: that I would like more opportunities to photograph him. To my surprise
I was informed shortly afterward that I
could fly with him and his family and
staff on the presidential helicopter from
San Clemente to El Toro Marine Base in
southern California.*

President and Mrs.
Nixon enjoying
their favorite view
at San Clemente.
January 1971.

*The president told me there was a bench
at San Clemente overlooking the Pacific
Ocean that was a favorite spot of his. He
asked if I would photograph him there with
his wife. After he resigned and returned to
San Clemente, I often saw the two of them
on this bench in my mind's eye, and I wondered what they must have thought as they
reflected on the highs and lows that life
had dealt them.*

RIGHT
President and Mrs.
Nixon on the beach
at San Clemente.
January 1971.

*Even though it was drizzling, the president
and Mrs. Nixon went for a walk along the
beachfront of their San Clemente retreat
and agreed to be photographed. It was a
challenge to capture the president in a
moment of relaxation, but here on the
beach the interplay between his wife and
him was both natural and affectionate.*

OPPOSITE, TOP
Mrs. Nixon in her bedroom at the White House, with her daughter, Julie (Mrs. David Eisenhower). February 1971.

Mrs. Nixon could not have been more pleasant to work with. After one session she asked me if I had gotten what I wanted, and when I told her I had, she said, "Good, why don't you relax; I have some wonderful homemade cookies."

OPPOSITE, BOTTOM
Julie Nixon Eisenhower working on needlepoint in the family quarters on the second floor of the White House. March 1970.

Despite what one felt about President Nixon, his two daughters, Julie and Tricia, were universally admired and were a tribute to their parents.

Martha Mitchell, the uninhibited wife of the attorney general, and her poodle, Buttons, telephoning from her Watergate apartment bedroom. March 1971.

I wanted to photograph Martha Mitchell on the telephone, because she was known for her frequent and revealing calls to women of the press corps. Since she preferred to speak to someone during the shot, I suggested she call my house. When our British au pair, Barbara, answered the phone, Mrs. Mitchell opened brightly with: "I guess you don't know who this is!" "No, who is it?" said Barbara, guardedly. "Martha Mitchell!" came the reply. Barbara quickly decided it was a hoax and retorted: "Oh yes, and this is the Queen Mother," and hung up.

Mrs. Nixon during a conversation with a journalist in the family quarters of the White House. February 1971.

Mrs. Nixon was being interviewed for a magazine story in the living room area of the family quarters on the second floor of the White House. Many women of the press shared my feeling that she was their favorite First Lady. Some of the questions amused her, and she laughed freely. However, when asked what had been the hardest time of her political life with the president, she said it was when he was defeated for the presidency in November 1960. She was devastated for all the people who had worked so hard on his behalf. At that moment she became very sad; I could see tears in her eyes.

Attorney General John Mitchell (right) and his wife, Martha (left), at a dinner party they gave for members of Nixon's administration in their Watergate apartment.
April 26, 1971.

The Mitchells were probably the most colorful couple in the Nixon administration, due in part to publicity Mrs. Mitchell generated. I did not know, until I arrived, who would attend the party and was delighted to have the chance to photograph such prominent members of the administration under such relaxed circumstances. After the guests left, Mitchell invited me to have a drink with him— a typical gesture from this generous and affable man.

Formal reception in the White House. February 1971.

Presidents of the United States do a lot of formal entertaining, and these receptions and dinners are always grand occasions. The Nixons carried on the tradition, changing only one small detail. They had served soup at the first state dinner, but because Nixon spilled some of it on his tuxedo, soup was never again to be on the menu! The press tended to dwell on the stiffness of the First Couple, but those who knew them better attributed it to their fundamental shyness.

H. R. Haldeman filming the arrival of British Prime Minister Edward Heath. December 17, 1970.

I often saw Haldeman with his 8mm movie camera. He loved filming President Nixon and the action around him at public appearances. On this occasion the prime minister was arriving on the south lawn of the White House for a state visit. I was on the White House balcony, and I glanced down. There was Haldeman, crew cut and all, shooting away. Years later, while I was having lunch in a restaurant, he stopped by my table and asked what had happened to all the pictures I had taken of the Nixon White House. I told him that I had them in storage. He suggested, "Why don't you and I do a book together?"

Kissinger with
secretaries in his
outer office in
the White House.
December 28, 1970.

*Gaining entrée
into inner sanc-
tums such as this
one was the most
difficult part;
once in, I was
usually ignored
and allowed to go
about my work.*

President Nixon
and Henry Kissinger
during an early
morning conference
by the Oval Office
door leading to
the Rose Garden.
February 10, 1971.

*The president and Kissinger were
constantly making news regarding
Vietnam, Cambodia, China, and other
foreign policy matters, and I was eager
to get a photograph that would symbolize
their close relationship. My patience
was rewarded one winter morning when,
ignoring my presence, the two men
conferred in the Oval Office.*

ABOVE
President Nixon
with (left to right)
John Ehrlichman,
Henry Kissinger,
and H. R. Haldeman,
in the Oval Office.
February 10, 1971.

OPPOSITE
President Nixon in
the Oval Office with
his top assistants—
(left to right) Henry
Kissinger, John
Ehrlichman, and
H. R. Haldeman.
February 10, 1971.

The doorway provided a perfect frame for this view of the Oval Office, as seen by an outsider looking in. I was not the only one who had difficulty gaining access to the Oval Office. Haldeman himself admitted to having constructed a protective wall around the president; some outsiders characterized it as a "Berlin Wall."

President Nixon with
aide Stephen Bull.
February 10, 1971.

*I loved being a fly on the wall in the Oval
Office, waiting for that perfect fleeting
moment. Steve Bull, the president's
appointments secretary, was gesturing to
someone as the president, with hands in
pockets, and with his own seemingly dark
thoughts, walked toward him.*

OPPOSITE, TOP
President Nixon
in the Oval Office
with aides Stephen
Bull, Henry
Kissinger, and
Robert Odle in the
background.
February 10, 1971.

*There are those
who maintain that
Nixon came to the
presidency better
prepared, in terms
of personnel and
organization, than
any president
before him. The
Nixon White House
appeared to operate
with strict control
and efficiency—a
fact that makes the
Watergate affair all
the more difficult
to explain.*

OPPOSITE, BOTTOM
President Nixon and
Rose Mary Woods,
the president's
personal secretary.
April 20, 1971.

*Rose Mary Woods
was catapulted into
history in 1973
when she said she
might be the person
responsible for the
mysterious erasing
of 18 1/2 minutes of
critical information
on key tapes of
conversations held
in the Oval Office
on June 20, 1972—
three days after
the Watergate
break-in. It does
not take long for
an anonymous
secretary to become
a household word
when implicated
in the questionable
doings of her boss.*

President Nixon in the Oval Office with H. R. Haldeman. February 10, 1971.

Haldeman said of his job: "I was rarely more than a few feet away from him during the working day and never out of immediate touch by telephone at any hour of the day or night. . . . I was the President's sounding board."

President Nixon
heads from the
White House to
his office in the
Executive Office
Building on an early
winter morning,
with his valet,
Manolo Sanchez.
Secret Service agents
are in front and
back. December
31, 1970.

*Every day I would arrive at the White
House early, on the off chance that there
would be something unexpected to photograph. On this chilly December morning,
I grabbed my camera and rushed outside
in time to photograph the president with
the omnipresent Secret Service men—one
in front and one behind, at a respectable
distance. Holding a large umbrella was
Manolo Sanchez, the president's personal
valet, who was from Spain and was very
proud that he—an immigrant—held such
a significant position. He was completely
devoted to the president and very friendly
with everyone.*

President Nixon
and Attorney
General John
Mitchell returning
to the Oval Office
after conferring on
the terrace outside.
April 20, 1971.

*The men ignored
my presence, so I
maintained a dis-
creet distance and
continued snap-
ping. Mitchell was
spoken of as the
president's closest
confidant, and the
series of pictures
I took that day
bore that out.*

Attorney General
John Mitchell
(left) and President
Nixon outside the
Oval Office.
April 20, 1971

*President Nixon
and John Mitchell
discuss matters on
the terrace outside
the Oval Office,
overlooking the
Rose Garden.*

THE **COMMITTEE**
TO **RE-ELECT**
THE **PRESIDENT**

PAGES 76–77
The Nixon White
House, taken from
the Washington
Monument.
May 1972.

RICHARD NIXON'S FIRST TERM IN THE WHITE HOUSE, though it embodied many successes, also brought him a number of galling setbacks. He failed to control the Supreme Court, even with an unusual number of nominations to its bench. He failed in the 1970 and 1972 elections to lead his party into dominance of Congress. By the end of that first term, his congressional support for carrying on the war in Vietnam was beginning to evaporate. He had promised to "bring us together" but some of his considered rhetoric and many of his impulsive statements had further divided the nation on the war issue.

With Kissinger's eager help, he had managed to take unprecedented personal control of foreign policy, but he nevertheless believed himself frustrated in a president's nominal control of the State Department and the Central Intelligence Agency. The Cold War, despite his efforts at détente—for which an anti-Nixon press was giving Kissinger an unfair share of the credit—still seemed intractable. Racial problems, even after the progress the administration had made on school desegregation, still plagued the nation—especially the issue of busing children to schools outside their neighborhoods, a process Nixon had vainly hoped to stop. The press, he was convinced without much real reason, remained his sworn enemy. He had appointed his personal hero, John Connally of Texas, as secretary of the Treasury, and he had wanted Connally (instead of the bumbling Spiro T. Agnew) as his 1972 running mate and probable successor in 1976. But other Republicans and Connally himself persuaded him that an apostate Democrat would not be accepted in either role.

Nixon had always seethed with internal anger at slights real and imagined and had expected, as president at last, to avenge himself against his enemies: liberals, reporters, antiwar activists, Kennedyites—"Nixon-haters" all. But that had not proved easy and he had been balked in this desire, too, in the hope he blatantly expressed: "They are asking for it, and they are going to get it."

It was perhaps for all these and no doubt other frustrations, as if they had been combined into one, that he had so frequently flailed at his perceived enemies and turned to action outside the law—electronic surveillance; infiltrating radical groups; briefly approving, then abandoning, the "Huston Plan" for "combating terrorism" by numerous illegal methods; and creating the "Plumbers," an unauthorized covert unit within the White House, designed supposedly to stop "leaks," but actually to carry out all sorts of intelligence gathering. With or without Nixon's specific knowledge, his agents had made illicit entries into Dr. Lewis Fielding's office in California and into the offices of the Democratic National Committee (D.N.C.) in Washington. When his aide Charles Colson talked of "firebombing" the Brookings Institution, the president did not demur.

Fatally, Nixon had turned his efforts for a second term over to the Committee to Re-elect the President, a name with two important implications. First, though the committee's planners had hoped it would be referred to as "the C.R.P.," almost inevitably the popular acronym, occasioning much derision, became CREEP; second, the title deliberately referred to "the President" rather than "Nixon." To some extent this may have been because Nixon knew he was not greatly loved and had resolved to focus on the official rather than the personal identity. Primarily, however, the name reflected Nixon's decision not to run as a Republican—not even to allow the party name to appear in his commercials, literature, and other campaign materials. His was not only a minority party, when he needed votes from all Americans; he also believed the people's respect for a sort of disembodied entity called "the President" exceeded its regard for either party or any personality.

The C.R.P., however, proved to be an unusual election manager. Under its auspices, a team headed by G. Gordon Liddy put into effect an expensive plan, ostensibly for political espionage, called Operation Gemstone. It was approved, at Key Biscayne in the spring of 1972, by Nixon's former law partner and first attorney general, John Mitchell, then chairman of the C.R.P., who may have been distracted at the time by the erratic behavior of his wife, Martha. The Gemstone team failed in its plan to rob the safe of Hank Greenspun, a Las Vegas publisher who was believed to have important documents that might disclose a Nixon connection with the billionaire Howard Hughes. But in May 1972, Gemstone's crew of Cuban burglars broke into the D.N.C. offices and planted wiretaps, notably on the phone of Chairman Lawrence O'Brien (a particular target of Nixon's animosity).

Mitchell soon complained that the wiretap information was worthless and the ever-eager Liddy promised to do better. On June 17, 1972, the Cubans and James McCord, security chief for the C.R.P., were caught and arrested in the D.N.C. offices in the Watergate Office Building. In the address books of two of the men apprehended was the name of Howard Hunt, who had been connected to the Nixon White House.

The Watergate scandal would follow as the night the day. But Nixon, who was in Key Biscayne and read about the arrests in the newspaper, maintained for nearly two years that he knew nothing about it. He probably had *not* known specifically about the break-in and certainly had not ordered it, but the stop-at-nothing, smash-our-enemies atmosphere he created in the White House probably influenced Mitchell in approving Gemstone and Liddy in conceiving and following it.

The C.R.P., moreover, put together a "dirty tricks" operation under one Donald Segretti, who had been a classmate at the University of Southern California with Dwight Chapin of the White House staff. Segretti, concealing the connection to the C.R.P. and the White House, organized a group of twenty-eight operatives in seventeen states, to a limited extent doing real intelligence work but mostly playing at—some schoolboyish, some effective—"dirty tricks." Segretti's tricksters forged letters on Democratic candidates' letterheads, got up false bumper stickers ("Help Muskie Bus More Children"), leaked falsehoods to the press, and disrupted Democratic schedules and meetings. In one memorable case, during the New Hampshire primary, they attributed racist remarks about French Canadians to Senator Edmund Muskie of Maine, then the Democratic front-runner, and cast aspersions on Mrs. Muskie. Emotionally defending himself and his wife during a television broadcast, Muskie broke down and cried—probably killing his presidential candidacy, which afterward faded away.

During the campaign, the Segretti operation and its connections in Washington were exposed by the Washington *Post* (though too late to save Edmund Muskie) and Segretti himself disappeared from any future political involvement. The "dirty tricks" had little real success, except to give an enduring shady aura to the Nixon campaign, as did the sweeping fundraising efforts on his behalf, led by Maurice Stans (the 1972 campaign raised $60 million and spent $56 million, huge amounts at the time; in 1968, Nixon had spent only $36.5 million).

Neither dirty tricks nor excessive fundraising, however, had the damaging effect of those arrests of the Gemstone burglars in the offices of the D.N.C. Richard Nixon began at once to insist that he knew nothing about such "bizarre behavior"—what he allowed his press secretary, Ronald Ziegler, to dismiss as a "third-rate burglary." Immediately, however, he began the cover-up from which there would be no turning back.

On June 23, 1972, with the election fast approaching, he approved a plan to have the C.I.A. label the Watergate break-in a matter of national security. This was calculated to provide the Federal Bureau of Investigation with a plausible reason for stopping or limiting its investigation; but the tape that recorded Nixon and Bob Haldeman discussing this misleading scheme, when later discovered, was the "smoking gun" that proved him guilty of obstruction of justice and ultimately would force his resignation.

John Mitchell (left),
chairman of the
Committee to Re-
elect the President
(C.R.P.), with Clark
MacGregor, congres-
sional liaison and
chairman of the
C.R.P. after Mitchell.
This was taken dur-
ing the transition
period. July 1972.

*I had already begun photographing behind
the scenes at the C.R.P. headquarters when
John Mitchell, the C.R.P.'s first chairman,
resigned shortly after the Watergate break-
in and Clark MacGregor took over. Martha
Mitchell had been publicly demanding that
her husband give up politics. Many high-
ranking aides were heartbroken, because
despite his dour public visage, Mitchell
was a friendly man who inspired enormous
respect and affection among his staff and
friends. I was always happy to see him—
although I don't know whether he was as
happy to see me photographing at the C.R.P.
right after the break-in. If he wasn't, he
never showed it.*

Jeb Stuart Magruder
—deputy campaign
director at the C.R.P..,
former Haldeman
aide, and deputy
director of White
House communica-
tions—in his office
during a morning
meeting with
members of his staff.
June 28, 1972.

*After the Watergate break-in, as suspicion
grew that the White House might be
involved, I jokingly said to Jeb Magruder,
"You guys will do anything for publicity."
Many people have expressed amazement
that I was allowed to photograph the C.R.P.,
considering what must have been going on
in the minds of those working there.*

OPPOSITE, TOP
Jeb Magruder's office
at the C.R.P. head-
quarters. Left to
right: Powell Moore,
deputy press director
of the C.R.P. and for-
mer White House
aide; Herbert L.
Porter, scheduling
director of the C.R.P.
and former aide
to Haldeman;
an unidentified
campaign worker;
and Magruder.
June 28, 1972.

*Jeb Magruder, the
second in
command of the
C.R.P., actually
managed the day-
to-day operations
of the campaign
until Clark Mac-
Gregor replaced
Mitchell as chair-
man in July 1972.*

OPPOSITE, BOTTOM
Phillip Joanou (left),
discussing advertis-
ing campaign materi-
als with Jeb
Magruder (center)
and an unidentified
campaign worker at
the C.R.P. headquar-
ters. July 1972.

*Jeb Magruder, a
public relations
specialist before
going to the White
House, wore many
hats at the C.R.P.
Besides overseeing
advertising mater-
ial, he was respon-
sible for public
relations, polling,
research, and
planning.*

ABOVE
Jeb Magruder in the
office of Charles W.
Colson, special coun-
sel to the president.
June 29, 1972.

*Jeb Magruder had a meeting scheduled
with Chuck Colson the week of June 26,
1972, a week or so after the break-in, and
agreed to let me come along and take some
photographs. Colson had not been fore-
warned, and when he saw me, he barked
at Magruder, "Why the — are you bringing
Maroon here?" This took me by surprise;
Colson had always been cooperative and
friendly toward me when I was covering the
White House the year before. However, I
did know that his in-house image was less
than lovable. A memo to his own staff
ended: "I will be expecting maximum out-
put from every member of the staff for
whom I have any responsibility. I will be
very intolerant of less than maximum out-
put. I am totally unconcerned about anything other than getting the job done. . . .
Let me point out that the statement in
last week's UPI story that I was once
reported to have said that I would 'walk
over my grandmother, if necessary' is
absolutely correct." Since I was already
there, Magruder persuaded Colson to let
me stay, albeit briefly.*

Robert C. Mardian
at his desk at the
C.R.P. headquarters.
July 3, 1972.

Robert Mardian, a former assistant attorney general under John Mitchell, was chief legal counsel to the C.R.P. He was always cooperative when I was around, despite what must have been enormous burdens placed on him after the discovery of the Watergate break-in. It was an event in which he had no direct involvement, but which, once he learned of it, thrust him into a position that he himself described as "being caught in quicksand."

Robert Odle, director of administration and personnel for the C.R.P., and former White House aide. With unidentified campaign worker. July 3, 1972.

I already knew a number of the people at the C.R.P. from the time I spent photographing in the White House. Bob Odle, who had worked in Herb Klein's office there, was now in charge of personnel at the C.R.P. He had an incredible memory and knew the names, titles, and the jobs of everyone working there.

Edward C. Nixon, the president's brother, talking with campaign aide Ann Dore. At right, Arthur Amolsch. In the background, an unidentified campaign worker. June 29, 1972.

I wandered freely throughout the C.R.P. headquarters seeking photographic subjects. No one needed to tell me that this man was President Nixon's brother. He never minded my presence, and unlike his brother, he was mild-mannered.

C.R.P. staffers Harold Fangboner, left, and Clifford Miller, right. July 3, 1972.

People in the C.R.P. offices were orderly and respectable looking, and they wore shirts and ties. The operations there had an efficient, businesslike air about them as if the office was in a bank.

Jack Ford (left),
son of the future
president, and Harry
Haldeman (right),
student interns, at
the C.R.P. July 6,
1972.

*Just as in other
walks of life, the
children of people
in politics are often
involved in their
parents' work. Off
in the back rooms
of the C.R.P. head-
quarters were the
children of high-
profile fathers
doing low-level
campaign tasks.*

BOTTOM
Birthday party.
Jan Ehrlichman
(lighting candles),
Harry Haldeman
(in back, at left),
Peter Ehrlichman
(to the left behind
Jan), and three
unidentified
campaign workers.
July 6, 1972.

*Despite the grim
mood in other areas
of the C.R.P. head-
quarters after the
Watergate break-in,
the young Republi-
cans working there
were blissfully
unaware of the
storm that was
brewing when they
took time out, less
than three weeks
later, to help cele-
brate a birthday of
one of their own.*

Campaign staffer
Mark Rosenker and
unknown associate
in the communica-
tions room.
June 29, 1972.

Security at the C.R.P. headquarters was
intense. There were recording stations, and
closed-circuit television monitored activity
throughout the C.R.P. offices. Plainclothes
guards were stationed unobtrusively near
reception areas. One C.R.P. worker was
reported to have said, "There's an awful
lot of paranoia around here."

OPPOSITE
Two unidentified
C.R.P. employees
feed the shredding
machine at the
C.R.P. headquarters.
June 29, 1972.

After the Water-
gate break-in,
newspapers and
magazines ran
articles referring
to the shredding
machine at the
C.R.P. as playing a
part in consigning
sensitive informa-
tion to oblivion.

President Nixon and
Vice President Agnew
during inaugural cere-
monies on the east
front of the Capitol.
January 1973.

Nixon won re-election
by a landslide, and
on his inauguration
day in 1973 he
appeared to be
embarking on a
successful second
term in office.

President Nixon's
inaugural address,
east front of the
Capitol. January
1973.

The pomp and cer-
emony of Nixon's
inauguration day
was only intermis-
sion time as the
Watergate break-in
was a time-bomb
waiting to explode.

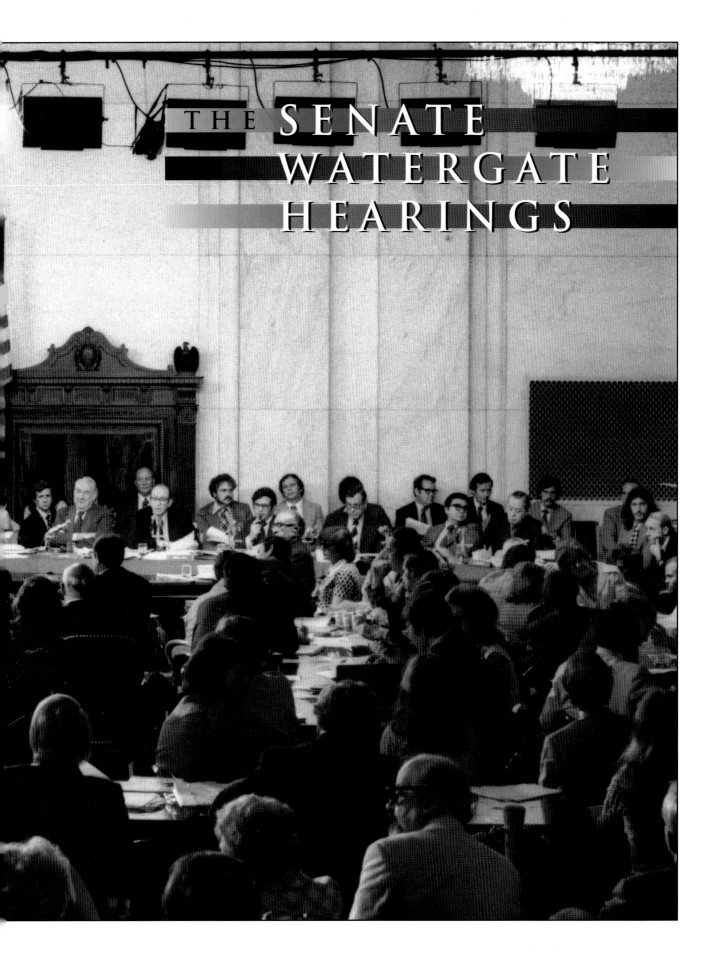

THE SENATE
WATERGATE
HEARINGS

O N June 25, 1973, some of the most damning testimony ever made against an incumbent president was delivered to the Senate Select Committee on Watergate by the youthful White House counsel, John Dean. Reading in a monotone from a prepared text, Dean asserted that Richard Nixon had had knowledge of a White House cover-up of the Watergate break-in since the day after the Cubans and James McCord were arrested in the D.N.C. offices. The president had discussed with him the possibilities of clemency and hush money for the burglars. Nixon's friend John Mitchell, the former attorney general and chairman of the C.R.P., had made cover-up payments to Howard Hunt. Nixon's principal aides, Bob Haldeman and John Ehrlichman, had orchestrated the plot and, with Nixon himself, tried to set up Mitchell to take all the blame. And it was only when Dean decided that he might himself become the "fall guy" for the president's men that he had started to cooperate with prosecutors.

Millions of stupefied Americans saw and heard Dean's startling testimony. The Senate Select Committee on Presidential Campaign Activities (which was most often called the Watergate Committee), and its Democratic chairman, Senator Sam J. Ervin Jr. of North Carolina, opened their hearings on May 17 to a television audience larger than that for Nixon's "Checkers" speech two decades earlier. The avuncular Ervin, a former state supreme court justice who preferred to be called "Judge," had stoutly refused White House efforts to keep television cameras out of committee sessions, and as witness after witness had described the seamier side of the Nixon administration, the nation watched in horrified fascination.

Dean provided the most detailed response to the repeated question of Howard Baker, the committee's ranking Republican: "What did the President know, and when did he know it?" But was Dean's story true? He provided no documentation and Nixon stood firmly on his previous denials. The committee hearings, however sensational, seemed at an impasse—until, on July 16, Alexander Butterfield, an aide to Haldeman, disclosed under questioning the existence of a secret, voice-activated White House taping system. Not only had Nixon's talks with foreign and other leaders been recorded, so had all the internal Watergate discussions, including those John Dean had described in such telling detail. The seven members of the committee and millions of watching Americans realized immediately that those secret tapes could verify Dean's story—or Nixon's—if they could be publicly heard.

John Russell Dean III,
staff assistant, in the
White House office of
Robert Finch, coun-
selor to the president.
September 17, 1970.

*This picture of John
Dean was pivotal
in my decision to
continue my photo-
graphic document
on Nixon. In the
week of April 2,
1973, a picture
researcher at
Time called to
ask whether I had
a picture of Dean
in my files. By the
time I located one,
the researcher had
called back several
times, each time
more urgently than
the last. I realized
something serious
was happening,
and sure enough,
this lonely looking,
contemplative man
became a key figure
in what was to
unfold.*

John Connally, among others, urged Nixon to burn the tapes, which were his personal property and had not yet been subpoenaed as evidence; he could explain that they contained "national security" secrets. But Nixon refused, making the fatal misjudgments that destroying the tapes would look like a guilty act, and that they would generally corroborate his account of events. Anyway, he believed the tapes were amply protected from the public and the courts by the principle of executive privilege he had seen Eisenhower use effectively against the demands of Senator Joseph McCarthy.

In further committee testimony, before a mesmerized national audience, Mitchell, Ehrlichman—belligerently—and Haldeman—smoothly—all stood foursquare behind Nixon's innocence of any involvement in Watergate or a cover-up. Mitchell attempted to rebut John Dean, charge by charge. Haldeman and Ehrlichman tried to blame Mitchell. But the existence of the president's tapes overwhelmed all other testimony; obviously they contained the crucial evidence.

The Watergate Committee, Special Prosecutor Archibald Cox, and Federal Judge John Sirica all demanded access to or subpoenaed the tapes. Nixon was hounded and apparently cornered by all three branches of government. But on grounds of executive privilege, the separation of powers, and national security, Nixon, with his demonstrated tenacity, refused them all though he issued selected fragments of the taped conversations to support his story. Finally, he announced an appeal of Judge Sirica's subpoena, a move that ultimately would bring the matter before the Supreme Court—four of whose nine justices, including Chief Justice Warren Burger, he had named. He would obey, Nixon said ambiguously, a "definitive ruling" by that court.

The Watergate Committee, still without the tapes, ended its hearings later that year. But in October 1973, Nixon—just after suffering the embarrassment of Vice President Agnew's resignation to avoid criminal charges—made another egregious misjudgment. He decided to fire Special Prosecutor Cox and return the Watergate investigation to the administration's own Justice Department. But Attorney General Elliot Richardson, who had appointed Cox, had promised the Senate that he would not fire the special prosecutor. Richardson, therefore, resigned rather than comply with Nixon's order. That same day his nominal successor, Assistant Attorney General William Ruckelshaus, also refused the president's directive, and also tried to

The hands of Richard Helms, former director of the Central Intelligence Agency, while testifying during the Senate Watergate Hearings. August 2, 1973.

Even the most outwardly composed witnesses at the hearings could not hide telltale signs of inner tension.

resign; Nixon fired him instead. Solicitor General Robert Bork, who was next in line to be attorney general, finally did the job—whereupon the nation exploded in astonishment and wrath at what was indelibly labeled the Saturday Night Massacre, an astounding miscalculation by a man known as a master politician.

John Chancellor, then the anchorman for NBC News, told another vast television audience that night that Richard Nixon had set off "what may be the most serious constitutional crisis in . . . history."

Senator Sam J. Ervin
Jr., chairman of
the Senate Select
Committee on
Presidential Cam-
paign Activities,
with Senator Howard
H. Baker Jr., vice
chairman, to his left.
May 23, 1973.

*As a counterpoint
to Senator Ervin,
the Republicans
had chosen Senator
Howard Baker of
Tennessee. Youth-
ful, energetic, and
photogenic, he
became famous
for his pointed
question during
the hearings, when
he asked, "What
did the president
know, and when
did he know it?"*

James McCord (left), former CIA agent and security chief for the C.R.P., talking with Terry Lenzner (center), deputy to Sam Dash, Democratic chief counsel, outside the Senate Caucus Room prior to testifying before the Senate Select Committee on Presidential Campaign Activities, called "the Watergate Committee." May 18, 1973.

James McCord was a twenty-year veteran of the CIA, the C.R.P.'s security coordinator, and one of the five "burglars" who broke into the headquarters of the D.N.C. in the Watergate on June 17, 1972 and was arrested. He was a lead-off witness, and, like other witnesses, had conversations with attorneys or even committee staff members prior to giving testimony.

James McCord
testifying before
the Watergate
Committee.
May 18, 1973.

*McCord was a
sensational witness
and electrified the
room as he told of
political pressure
from the White
House and an offer
of executive
clemency if he
agreed to plead
guilty and remain
silent about the
Watergate break-in.
He refused the
offer, preferring to
play it straight and
let the chips fall
where they may.
At that moment
the Watergate
cover-up was
doomed. He was a
marvelous subject,
but capturing the
expression to match
the content of his
words required
one voice in my
head focusing on
every fleeting
visual moment and
another voice trig-
gering my finger
when the moment
was right.*

Jack Germond of
the Baltimore *Sun*.
May 18, 1973.

*There were four
major groups at the
Watergate hearings:
the committee, the
witnesses, the press,
and the spectators.
After the specta-
tors, the members
of the press were
the largest presence
in the room. Most
of them were daily
regulars, represent-
ing all the major
newspapers in the
country.*

The photographic
press corps was at
the hearings en
masse daily.
May 23, 1973.

*A regular contingent of photographers representing all the major
wire services, newspapers, and magazines gathered in the Caucus
Room every day. Almost all were members of the White House News
Photographers Association—old pros—who covered the White House
regularly when they weren't at the hearings. They respected each
other and knew how to work together and yet were fiercely competi-
tive. Newcomers, however aggressive, usually found themselves at
the back of the pack, and woe to local photographers on the road who
thought they, too, had rights. The pros knew when a certain gesture
or expression would make a good photograph; all their shutters and
motor drives would start clicking noisily at once. And, on another
matter, they were unanimous: they informally voted Maureen Dean
the woman for whom they would most like to borrow $5,000 to
take on a honeymoon. John Dean, her husband, had testified
regarding $15,200 in cash in his custody in his White House safe:
"I removed a packet of bills amounting to $4,850 and placed my
personal check for that amount with the remaining cash . . . to pay
for the anticipated expenses of my wedding and honeymoon."*

Sally Harmony
during testimony
before the Watergate
Committee.
June 5, 1973.

Sally Harmony, Gordon Liddy's secretary, was an exception—a female witness called to testify. She and Liddy were sometimes referred to as "James Bond and Miss Moneypenny." Liddy pleaded guilty to the Watergate break-in and refused to testify before the Watergate grand jury. Harmony did testify, and when she was asked why she was good at what she did, she answered with a half smile, "I can keep a secret."

Robert Reisner,
youth coordinator
for the C.R.P.
June 5, 1973.

One by one came the parade of sad young men caught in the web created by loyalty to their superiors or to the peer pressure of wanting to be a team player. I had traveled with Robert Reisner on the campaign trail when I was photographing at the C.R.P. When he saw me and I explained why I was there, he commented that he was glad for me, but sad for himself.

Jack Caulfield, a former New York City detective, was also a security coordinator at the C.R.P. He testified that he met with McCord on several occasions and carried offers of executive clemency from the very highest levels of the White House. He, McCord, and Tony Ulasewicz lent a Runyonesque air of cops and robbers to the hearings. There were truly humorous aspects to the intrigue, and for a while the hearings bordered on entertainment. Some of the witnesses appearing before the committee were a Hollywood casting agent's dream.

John Caulfield (right), ex-detective, and his lawyer, John P. Sears, prior to testifying. May 23, 1973.

Newsman catnapping
during a break in the
hearings. June 5,
1973.

*Covering the hearings wasn't always grand
theater. There were lulls (and lullabies!),
and especially in the afternoon, some hard-
working newsmen were found to be not so
much "out to lunch" as "out from lunch."*

OPPOSITE
Mary McGrory of the
Washington *Evening
Star,* on a public
telephone outside
the Senate Caucus
Room. June 6, 1973.

*Since writers and
reporters did not
have cell phones
in 1973, one of the
principal means
of communication
were the pay
phones in the
Senate corridors.*

Senator Edward
Gurney, of Florida
(left), and Deputy
Minority Counsel
Fred D. Thompson.
May 23, 1973.

*Senator Gurney was a Nixon loyalist, and
his attitudes toward the witnesses reflected
those sympathies. Some of John Dean's
allegations met with their harshest scrutiny
from Senator Gurney. Gurney was concerned that the hearings were taking too
long, resulting in damage to the country
and its reputation abroad.*

Some controversy and embarrassment
erupted during Ehrlichman's testimony
when Senator Inouye's microphone, which
he believed to be switched off, picked up
a remark that most of the press reported
as: "What a liar!" Inouye maintained
that he had said "What a lawyer!"

Senators Daniel K.
Inouye (Hawaii), left,
and Joseph M. Montoya
(New Mexico). June 7,
1973.

Left to right: Senator
Herman E. Talmadge
(Georgia); Senator
Daniel K. Inouye;
Senator Joseph M.
Montoya. June 14,
1973.

*The end of the committee table on the
Democrat's side included Senator
Talmadge, one of the shrewdest men in
the Senate, Senator Inouye, considered the
Democrat's most penetrating questioner,
and Senator Montoya. Among the press
Montoya was called the "room clearer"
because of his colorless manner; however,
he terrified the witnesses' lawyers with his
unpredictable, yet often loaded, questions.*

Senator Herman
Talmadge of Georgia.
June 27, 1973.

*Senator Talmadge was a reluctant member
of the Watergate Committee, but the
Democratic majority leader, Senator Mike
Mansfield, insisted that he take part.
Although Senator Talmadge did not speak
much, his questions were perceptive and
went straight to the heart of the witness's
testimony. He said he saw himself as a
juror, and a good one he was.*

Jeb Magruder (right),
chief of staff and
deputy director of
the C.R.P., with his
wife, Gail, prior to
testifying.

*I had known the Magruders from the time
I was covering the White House in 1970–71.
In those happier times he was a deputy to
Herb Klein, Nixon's director of communications. Then, all appeared bright and promis-
ing for them. To see them here on the day he
was to start testifying was to see the anguish
of the situation etched on their faces.*

OPPOSITE
Maureen ("Mo")
Dean, wife of John
Dean, during her
husband's testimony.
June 25, 1973.

*More often than not wives of witnesses
accompanied their husbands. One of the
more glamorous and photogenic was
Maureen Dean, and a goodly supply of
Kodak film was exposed capturing her
cool composure. She returned the favor
by appearing camera-ready on each of
the four days her husband testified.*

John Dean (right)
and Maureen Dean
(center) in the Senate
Caucus Room, prior
to his testimony.
June 25, 1973.

*John Dean was the
White House insider
who talked—and
talked—and talked.
When he spotted me
on the first day of
his testimony, he
came over during
a recess and asked,
"How do I know
you? You look famil-
iar." I reminded
him that I had
photographed him
in the White House
two years earlier.
"Oh, yes," he said,
and walked away.
End of conversation.
But brief though it
was, it did not go
unrecorded by the
ever-present televi-
sion cameras, and
that night several
friends telephoned
me at home,
wanting to know
what John Dean
and I had been
talking about.*

Maurice Stans,
director and
chairman of the
finance committee
of the C.R.P.
June 12–13, 1973.

I had photographed Maurice Stans a number of years earlier when he was the budget director during the Eisenhower administration. He was successful, polished, good-looking, and always impeccably dressed. For two days he was grilled by the committee about his role as director and chairman of the finance committee of the C.R.P. He maintained his innocence of wrongdoing regarding cash disbursements of C.R.P. funds to Watergate burglar Bernard L. Barker and to Gordon Liddy, and the destruction of financial records after the break-in. No one seemed to annoy the Watergate Committee members as

much as Stans did, with his repeated disclaimers of any knowledge of the matters the members wished to address. At the same time, it struck me that even a man of his stature can appear vulnerable when called upon to respond to not just one, but a whole panel of accusers, and with the unforgiving eye of the television camera placing him in every living room in America. In an unguarded moment a person's reputation can be changed forever. At the conclusion of his testimony, Stans asked the committee if they would give him back "his good name" when they wrote their report.

Robert C. Mardian (left), chief legal counsel to the C.R.P., conferring with his lawyer, David Bress, during a break. June 19, 1973.

The days of the hearings would often be long, and during the periodic recesses witnesses used the time to smoke, review with their lawyers what had been said, and prepare for what was to follow.

West entrance to the Russell Senate Office Building, showing the Caucus Room on the upper level, and spectators lining up below to get into the hearings. July 11, 1973.

All day, every day, from May 17, 1973, to November 15, 1973, this was the scene in the Russell Senate Office Building, as people from all walks of life awaited their turn for admission to one of the prized spectator sports of the century.

OPPOSITE
Spectators during
the hearings,
including John
Lennon and
Yoko Ono.
June 26, 1973.

*It was not unusual
for superstars to
be part of the daily
crowd of specta-
tors. Years later,
this photograph is
perhaps the most
noteworthy of my
entire Watergate
collection to a
certain age group,
especially my own
children, who grew
up listening to the
Beatles.*

Spectators during
the hearings.
June 26, 1973.

*For the average American citizen, watching one's government in
action is both a right and a duty. Men and women of all ages,
from every walk of life and every region of the country, filled every
available seat and all the standing room at the back. It was better
entertainment than any theater; it was real, and it was free. It was
one thing to watch it on television, but far more compelling to be
there in person. Except, of course, when things got dull.*

Newscaster Douglas Kiker (with earphones) and a colleague during hearings. July 10, 1973.

The hearings entertained Americans, replacing soap operas or movie reruns—it was all live from the nation's capital, and it was reported by every medium known to modern communications: newspapers, magazines, radio, and television.

Norman Mailer during a break while covering the hearings as a member of the press corps. June 26, 1973.

The drama of the Watergate hearings attracted many high-profile writers and observers of the American scene to the daily ritual in the Senate Caucus Room. Despite the extensive coverage by television and the newspapers, one still had to be there to experience the full impact of what was happening.

"Sources," in this case Sam Dash, got the rapt attention of the Watergate scribes. Some of the important players in the daily drama were the people reporting it. To young journalists, covering the Watergate hearings was like being in combat is to the military. It could be their baptism by fire and a ladder for professional advancement.

Samuel Dash (center with glasses), chief counsel and staff director, briefs journalists during testimony. On the left are Miles Benson, Carl Bernstein, and Bob Jackson, and on the right Lesley Stahl, an unidentified woman, and Josh Darsa. June 26, 1973.

John Mitchell, former attorney general in the Nixon administration, later chairman of the C.R.P., and close personal friend and former law partner of Nixon, arriving on the first day of his testimony with the press out in force. July 10, 1973.

Under other circumstances, any member of the administration would have loved to generate the kind of attention they received as witnesses before the Watergate Committee.

John Mitchell
testified before the
Senate Watergate
Committee for
three days, July
10–12, 1973.

Mitchell was well-
liked by his staff,
and from the time
I spent with him
taking photographs,
I could understand
why. The Watergate
Committee, how-
ever, was not run-
ning a personalty
contest, and despite
his closeness to so
many people, he was
very much alone
when committee
members grilled
him about his ver-
sion of the events.

John Mitchell being
sworn in before the
Watergate Commit-
tee. July 10, 1973.

Before taking his oath as a witness,
John Mitchell was the focus of a feeding
frenzy by the press. During a lull in the
proceedings he spotted me in the crowd,
and asked what I was doing there. I told
him I was continuing my photographic
record of the Nixon era, and asked
whether he did not agree that what was
happening was of some moment. With the
usual twinkle in his eye he responded,
"I hope it's a fleeting one, Fred."

At a lunch break
during his testimony,
John Mitchell con-
fers with his lawyers.
Left to right: Marvin
Segal, William
Hundley, Mitchell,
and Plato Cacheris.
July 11, 1973.

*Mitchell testified for three days, and during one of their lunch
breaks, he allowed me to photograph him and his lawyers. For once
I was on the inside of the security ring that shielded witnesses as
they came and went from the committee room. They had a carry-
in lunch in a bare, windowless room in the basement below the
Senate Caucus Room; it could have been a scene from a Kafka
novel. After lunch they reviewed how the morning went, read
telegrams of encouragement sent to the former attorney general,
and tried to anticipate the afternoon's questioning.*

BELOW
At the end of John
Mitchell's second
day of testimony,
he and his attorneys,
Hundley and Cacheris,
return to the Hotel
Washington in their
limousine. July 11,
1973.

*At the conclusion of
the day's testimony
I was allowed to
accompany Mitchell
and two of his
lawyers in their
limousine back to
the Hotel Washing-
ton, where he was
staying. It was a
somber journey. I
sat in the front seat
with the driver and
with a very wide
15mm Hologon lens
on a Leica M was
able to squeeze off
an exposure or two.*

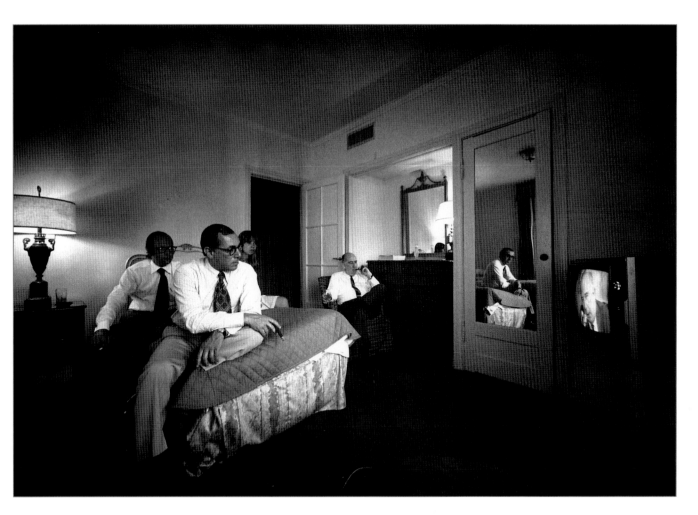

Mitchell and his lawyers held an evening strategy session in Mitchell's hotel suite, and afterward he and others looked at highlights of his testimony that day on the evening news. In spite of the implications and seriousness of Mitchell's situation, he was cool and unemotional, even introducing levity from time to time. Whatever was happening to him did not show on the outside, at least while I was there.

John Mitchell and attorney Marvin Segal (sitting on the bed in front of his son, Jack Mitchell, and his secretary, Sandra Hobbs), watching the day's testimony on television in his bedroom at the hotel. July 11, 1973.

Alexander Butterfield
arriving to testify.
July 16, 1973.

*Reporters covering
the hearings came
back after lunch
on July 16, 1973,
to word that some-
thing important
was going to be
disclosed by way of
a surprise witness.
Alexander Butter-
field, whom I had
known from the
White House when
he was deputy to
Haldeman and
secretary to the
cabinet, was in the
Caucus Room wait-
ing to testify. He
was sworn in, and
then, under ques-
tioning, dropped
his bombshell:
everything said in
President Nixon's
office was taped at
all times by a
voice-activated
recording set-up.
Butterfield was a
loyalist; it must
have wounded him
deeply to have to
be the one to give
this information to
the committee.*

Herbert W. Kalmbach was President Nixon's personal attorney, and for a time was responsible for getting hush money to the "burglars" and their families. Kalmbach had been waiting to testify when Alexander Butterfield gave his stunning testimony. They greeted each other as Butterfield took center stage.

Herbert W. Kalmbach (left), associate finance chairman of the C.R.P. under Maurice Stans, and his attorney, James O'Connor (right), listen to Terry Lenzner (center). July 16, 1973.

John D. Ehrlichman, chief domestic affairs adviser to the president. July 24, 1973.

John Ehrlichman could present a ferocious look at times. He had an extraordinarily mobile face, and I thought this photograph exactly captured his demeanor before the committee. He was combative and evasive, and came prepared to take on the committee. I had experienced his toughness in the White House, but there it was interspersed with humor and warmth. Before the committee the unvarnished version of John Ehrlichman was on display.

H. R. ("Bob.")
Haldeman, White
House chief of staff.
July 30, 1973.

*Bob Haldeman,
known as "Mr.
Inside," was per-
haps the most
inaccessible of all
the president's key
advisers. In his
1978 memoir,* The
Ends of Power,
*Haldeman wrote,
"Every president
needs an S.O.B.,
and I'm Nixon's."
His testimony
before the commit-
tee essentially mir-
rored Ehrlichman's
in content; both
men had the same
lawyer. Their
styles, however,
were quite differ-
ent: he was defer-
ential where
Ehrlichman was
pugnacious. Halde-
man seemed to be
the quintessential
advertising execu-
tive, talking only
about the positive
aspects of his
"product" and
admitting nothing
about the negative.*

ABOVE
Anthony Ulasewicz,
an associate of John
Caulfield who carried
messages from Dean
to McCord. July 18,
1973.

Some of the funniest moments occurred when Tony Ulasewicz, a former New York City cop and Kalmbach's delivery agent for the hush money, appeared before the committee. In his dry, deadpan New York accent Ulasewicz told about the trouble he had had trying to get lawyers to take off his hands $75,000, which he carried around in a hotel laundry bag. So often did he need to telephone "Callback Kalmbach" (he had trouble reaching him) for instructions that he began wearing a coin dispenser around his waist so that he would never run out of dimes. He was so disarmingly frank about the dark world of money drops, code names, and informants, that he was supplying more comic relief than the committee felt proper, and his appearances before it were curtailed.

OPPOSITE
L. Patrick Gray III,
acting director of
the F.B.I. until, on
April 27, 1973, he
suddenly resigned.
August 3, 1973.

Gray was probably the most pathetic high-level figure in the Watergate tragedy. When he failed in his bid to win confirmation as director of the F.B.I., Ehrlichman wasted no sympathy on him, saying, "Let him hang there . . . let him twist slowly, slowly in the wind." During his testimony he admitted burning documents given to him by John Dean—a criminal offense.

Richard Helms, director of the C.I.A. until his resignation at the president's request to become ambassador to Iran. August 2, 1973.

As the former head of the C.I.A., Helms was circumspect in the extreme in responding to the committee's questions, but was adamant in maintaining that he refused Haldeman's and Ehrlichman's request for the C.I.A.'s help in the Watergate affair. At one point he vented his exasperation: "The message doesn't seem to get across. The Agency had nothing to do with the Watergate break-in. Can all the newsmen in the room hear me now?"

Howard Hunt, along with James McCord and Gordon Liddy, the counsel to the finance committee for the C.R.P., was one of the leaders of the plot to break into the D.N.C. headquarters. A long-time C.I.A. agent and the chief operations officer at the ill-fated Bay of Pigs invasion, he had served as security chief of the C.R.P. Hunt had requested of Chairman Ervin that no photographers be allowed between him and the committee while he testified. Although most of the photographers left the room, I stayed and went to the far wall of the committee room, where I could still see Hunt. I put a 400mm telephoto lens on my Leica R, and squeezed off exposures at will.

Howard Hunt (right), talking with his lawyer, Sidney S. Sachs, during testimony before the Watergate Committee. September 24, 1973.

OPPOSITE
Senator Lowell
P. Weicker Jr.
July 30, 1973.

*Lowell Weicker of Connecticut was cut
from the old cloth of a fiery politician.
When he spoke, everyone paid attention,
not only for what he said but for how he
said it. He provided high theater for the
television audience, which had front-row
seats during the entire course of the hearings. Two television cameras above his
head took their aim at witnesses; Weicker
himself took a deadlier aim, blasting away
mercilessly at Haldeman, Ehrlichman,
and others, making it impossible for
them to explain away their behavior.*

Minority Counsel
Fred D. Thompson
(left) speaking with
Howard Baker Jr.
during hearing.
September 24, 1973.

*Senator Baker chose another Tennessean,
Fred Thompson, as chief minority counsel.
Only thirty years old, this was Thompson's
introduction to the big time. Even then he
had the characteristic deep voice and slow
drawl of a southern politician. His success
as a television personality during the hearings helped propel him into a career in
Hollywood, which, in turn, gave him the
exposure that helped him to capture his
own Senate seat in the 1990s.*

Patrick Buchanan, presidential speech writer and adviser, testifying. September 26, 1973.

I had known Patrick Buchanan as a friendly and cooperative person whenever he was a subject for my camera in the White House and on the campaign trail. Unlike many other White House personalities, he came to the hearings prepared to do battle, and was in an attack mode from the minute he began reading his prepared statement. For a while it appeared as though he had turned the tables on the committee: he was the inquisitor, and they the accused. Buchanan alleged that the

press had used leaks from the committee to smear him prior to his appearance, and he was not going to take it lying down. Never backing off, he made neither a confession nor an apology to the committee. The New York Times suggested that he made the members look "like a bunch of nit-pickers." When asked about his rules of conduct in political combat, he described them as "anything that was not immoral, unethical, illegal, or unprecedented in previous Democratic campaigns."

Donald H. Segretti (right), former classmate of White House staffers Dwight Chapin and Gordon Strachan, with his attorney, Victor Sherman, during testimony. October 3, 1973.

A number of people involved in the Watergate scandal could justifiably claim the title of "Mr. Dirty Tricks," and Donald Segretti was one of them. Among his alleged activities was the political sabotage of Democratic candidates during the 1972 election campaign. Photographing him whispering to his lawyer seemed to symbolize perfectly that role.

Ervin, seventy-five years old at the time of his chairmanship and a senator for eighteen years, had been the author of the resolution that proposed the investigation into the Watergate affair. He quickly became a household name as a result of his manner and approach, and developed such a following that spectators would applaud when he entered the room. Before coming to the Senate he had been a lower court and state supreme court judge for a total of fourteen years. To many, when he banged his gavel, he embodied the conscience of the nation. At the conclusion of the hearings it was evident to all that he had served his country and himself well.

Senator Sam J. Ervin Jr., chairman of the Watergate Committee. November 1, 1973.

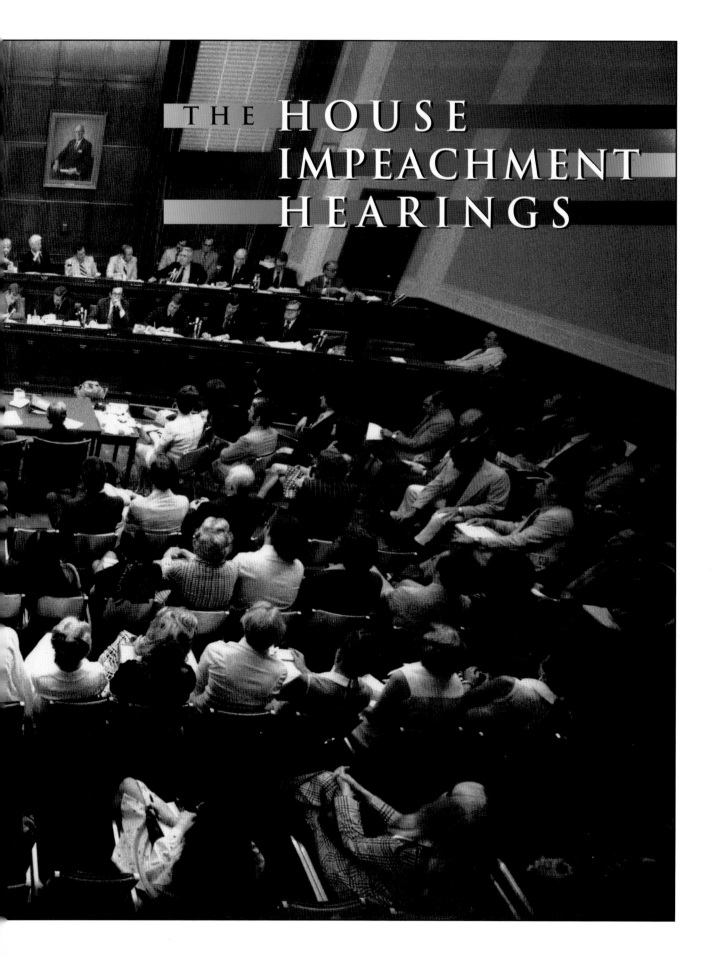

THE HOUSE IMPEACHMENT HEARINGS

PAGES 148–149
The House Judiciary
Committee Room
in the Sam Rayburn
House Office Building
during impeachment
proceedings. July
1974.

*The next chapter
in the unfolding
political tragedy
that was Watergate
was the impeach-
ment hearings in
the House Judiciary
Committee Room.
These hearings
opened on May 9,
1974, and were not
conducted like the
Watergate hearings.
Accredited photog-
raphers did not
have the free access
that we enjoyed in
the Senate Caucus
Room. Instead,
photographers were
rotated in, and once
in, we could not
station ourselves
between the com-
mittee members
and their counsels.
Nor could we freely
roam, except during
recesses. We had to
choose an unobtru-
sive location and
then stay there.*

Through the long winter and spring of 1973–74, Watergate and the Nixon tapes continued to command the nation's attention. No matter which way the president turned, despite his every effort to bring his ordeal to an end—he even fired Haldeman and Ehrlichman, "two of the finest public servants I have ever known"—he could not escape his vulnerability. Trying to evade court orders, Nixon desperately issued sanitized transcripts of many tapes. That mainly brought him public ridicule because of the many "expletive deleted" insertions that signaled how profane his actual language had been. Moreover, the Saturday Night Massacre had availed him little because a new special prosecutor, Leon Jaworski, continued Archibald Cox's determined quest for the tapes themselves.

The House Judiciary Committee opened hearings on May 9, 1974, to determine whether to recommend that Richard Nixon be impeached. Already on April 11, the committee had subpoenaed forty-two of the Nixon tapes, with only three members voting nay—including Trent Lott of Mississippi, who was to become Senate majority leader more than twenty years later. That spring, Nixon's summit with Leonid Brezhnev in the Soviet Union made no real headlines and failed to quell his mounting problems at home. He returned to the United States on July 8, the very day the Supreme Court (minus Justice William Rehnquist, a Nixon nominee, who had recused himself because he had previously served in the Nixon Justice Department) heard arguments on Nixon's appeal to Sirica's subpoena for a number of his tapes.

Obviously, it was to be a long, hard summer for the president and his dwindling band of loyalists. As was predictable, hard blows fell promptly. On July 24, the House Judiciary Committee's sessions began to appear on television, attracting, as had the Senate's Watergate Committee the year before, a massive audience. Ninety percent of the American people heard some part of the four-day committee debate on impeachment.

That day, too—July 24—Warren Burger, whom Nixon himself had nominated for chief justice, read a unanimous Supreme Court ruling that executive privilege could not cover evidence in a criminal case. Nixon would have to turn over the subpoenaed tapes to Special Prosecutor Jaworski. Accordingly, on August 5, the White House released full transcripts, including one containing the incriminating "smoking gun" conversation between Nixon and Haldeman on June 23, 1972.

Meanwhile, the Judiciary Committee had voted on July 27, 1974, to approve an article of impeachment charging Nixon with obstruction of justice. On July 29, it adopted another charge—that Nixon had abused presidential powers, including attempts to use the Internal Revenue Service to harass his "enemies." Still a third charge—that Nixon had refused to comply with the committee's subpoenas for his tapes—was approved on July 30. (Significantly, however, the committee rejected, 26 to 12, a charge dealing with the secret bombing of Cambodia in 1969; Congress will seldom, perhaps never, condemn a president for actions he takes as commander-in-chief of the armed forces.)

It was the "smoking gun" tape, however, that devastated any small remaining chance that Richard Nixon could survive as president. When it became public on August 5, making it clear that Nixon had been lying to friends, family, colleagues, Congress, and the public for more than two years, and proving incontrovertibly the obstruction of justice charge, what was left of his public and political support disintegrated. The ten Judiciary Committee Republicans who had voted against every article of impeachment all reversed themselves; even Vice President Ford said he could no longer repeat his accustomed defense of the president. The thirty-four Senate votes Nixon had counted on for acquittal of impeachment charges shrank to only "seven certain," in a head count by a Nixon aide. Polls showed overwhelming national sentiment for the president's resignation or removal.

It only remained for Barry Goldwater and two Republican colleagues, Senate Minority Leader Hugh Scott and House Minority Leader John Rhodes, to call on Nixon and inform him officially that he did not have enough support in the Senate—fifteen votes at best, Scott guessed, less than half enough to win acquittal in a two-thirds roll call. To reporters outside, however, the three Republicans did not tell what by then they knew: that even the indomitable Richard Nixon had surrendered and would resign the presidency.

Goldwater said sadly: "We were fond old friends talking over a very painful situation." And in response to a question whether the House would vote on impeachment if the president resigned, Rhodes replied, "No useful purpose would be served by that." Resignation would finish the impeachment process.

On the night of August 8, 1974, having absorbed all these body blows, Richard Nixon went before the television cameras, as he had done so often, but this time, not in triumph or defiance. "I shall resign the presidency," he told an estimated 110 million watching Americans, "effective at noon tomorrow."

Henry Kissinger, ever the courtier, assured Nixon after the sixteen-minute speech was over, that history would rank him as one of the great presidents. Richard Nixon, ever the cynic about his judges, replied, "That depends, Henry, on who writes the history."

President Nixon
arrives for what is
to be his last State
of the Union
address to Congress.
January 30, 1974.

*Nixon's last
address to the
nation came
between the Water-
gate hearings and
the impeachment
hearings. The con-
spicuous congenial-
ity between the
president and the
Democratic leaders
of Congress as he
made his way
through the House
chamber made it
hard to imagine
that seven months
later Nixon would
resign in disgrace.*

The House Judiciary Committee Room in the Sam Rayburn House Office Building during impeachment proceedings. July 1974.

The House Judiciary Committee was much larger than the Senate Watergate Committee, and its members, instead of being behind one long table, had seats on two levels. Using a Widelux camera, which uses two 35mm film frames for one image, this long-version image was possible.

House Judiciary Committee. Front row, left to right: Representatives George E. Danielson (California), James R. Mann (South Carolina), Elizabeth Holtzman (New York), Wayne Owens (Utah), Lawrence J. Hogan (Maryland). Second row, left to right: Representatives Don Edwards (California), Robert W. Kastenmeier (Wisconsin), Jack B. Brooks (Texas), Harold D. Donohoe (Massachusetts), Peter W. Rodino Jr. (New Jersey), Edward Hutchinson (Michigan), Robert McClory (Illinois), Trent Lott (Mississippi), Henry P. Smith (New York). July 1974.

Chairman Peter Rodino, like his counterpart in the Senate, Sam Ervin, ran the hearings in a nonpartisan and dignified manner. They became a model of how to run such otherwise politically divisive inquiries. Absent were the more colorful witnesses of the Senate hearings, but this was the endgame—the moment of truth for the president.

Chairman Rodino
with Representative
David W. Dennis of
Indiana. July 1974.

*In the closing days,
the hearings took
on an increasingly
grim mood as the
vote on the articles
of impeachment
approached.*

Representative
Barbara Jordan.
July 1974.

*One of the giants
during the impeach-
ment hearings was
Barbara Jordan of
Texas, who stood
out not only for
the manner and
tone of her delivery
but also for her
unswerving focus.
She gained national
prominence with
her simple but pow-
erful assertion:
"My faith in the
Constitution is
whole. It is com-
plete. It is total."*

John Doar (left),
special counsel to
the House Judiciary
Committee, talks with
Elizabeth Holtzman.
July 1974.

*The only time it was possible to get candid
photographs of people relating to each other
at the impeachment hearings was
during the recesses.*

John Doar was Rodino's chief counsel, and his job was to present a case to the committee that would support a vote for impeachment. This was lawyerly work; not visually dramatic but potentially devastating to the Nixon presidency.

John Doar (center) talking with Albert E. Jenner Jr. (right), nominal minority counsel. Francis O'Brien (left), chief of staff to Chairman Rodino. July 1974.

OPPOSITE
Left to right, committee staffers Bernard Nussbaum, Evan Davis (seated), Hillary Rodham, and an unidentified man during a break in the impeachment proceedings in the House Judiciary Committee Room. July 1974.

Just as in the Senate hearings, many bright young lawyers gained valuable experience that served them well in their future careers. Some of the little known men and women seen in photographs taken during the Nixon era have become household names—particularly the future First Lady, Hillary Rodham Clinton.

ABOVE
Members of the press corps. Left to right in foreground: Ray Scherer, John Chancellor, Peter Hackes, and Art Buchwald. July 1974.

As during the Senate Watergate hearings, the impeachment hearings attracted a contingent of press personalities whose faces reflect the compelling nature of what they were witnessing.

PAGES 164–165
During a recess in the hearings, Trent Lott is interviewed by Sam Donaldson and Frank Reynolds of ABC, in the lobby. July 1974.

Most of the press were set up outside the committee's hearing room. On July 27, 1974, after the committee voted 27 to 11 to recommend passage of the first of the articles of impeachment, the news was broadcast to the waiting world. It was the first recommendation of impeachment to be lodged against a president by a House investigating body since 1868.

ROLL CALL

DATE 7/29/74

No. _____ H. _____ S. _____

ARTICLE II

	COMMITTEE	Ayes	Nays	Present	Ayes	Nays
Present		✓				
	MR. DONOHUE	✓				
	MR. BROOKS	✓				
	MR. KASTENMEIER	✓				
	MR. EDWARDS	✓				
	MR. HUNGATE	✓				
	MR. CONYERS	✓				
	MR. EILBERG	✓				
	MR. WALDIE	✓				
	MR. FLOWERS	✓				
	MR. MANN	✓				
	MR. SARBANES	✓				
	MR. SEIBERLING	✓				
	MR. DANIELSON	✓				
	MR. DRINAN	✓				
	MR. RANGEL	✓				
	MS. JORDAN	✓				
	MR. THORNTON	✓				
	MS. HOLTZMAN	✓				
	MR. OWENS	✓				
	MR. MEZVINSKY					
	MR. HUTCHINSON		✓			
	MR. McCLORY			✓		
	MR. SMITH			✓		
	MR. SANDMAN		✓			
	MR. RAILSBACK			✓		
	MR. WIGGINS			✓		
	MR. DENNIS		✓			
	MR. FISH			✓		
	MR. MAYNE		✓			
	MR. HOGAN		✓			
	MR. BUTLER		✓			
	MR. COHEN			✓		
	MR. LOTT		✓			
	MR. FROEHLICH			✓		
	MR. MOORHEAD			✓		
	MR. MARAZITI			✓		
	MR. LATTA					
	MR. RODINO, *Chairman*		✓			
	TOTAL	28	10			

THE FINAL DAYS

*I*N THE MONTH AFTER NIXON'S RETURN FROM THE SOVIET UNION on July 8 until he announced his resignation on August 8, he vacillated —physically, between the White House and his estate at San Clemente in California; mentally, between resignation and fighting on (or *how* to fight on); spiritually, between despair and resolution; and practically, between the best interests of the nation and those of Richard Nixon. If he resigned, he knew, he would rate a $60,000 annual pension and $96,000 a year for staff. But if he were impeached and removed from office, he would sacrifice it all.

Only his wife, Pat; daughters, Tricia and Julie; and their husbands, Edward Cox and David Eisenhower, retained unquestioning faith in him; they didn't know, that summer, about the "smoking gun" tape until it became public on August 5. By the end of the televised Judiciary Committee hearings, a poll showed the public to be in favor of impeachment, 66 to 27 percent—and at that time the public didn't know about that "smoking gun" either.

Other Republicans and Nixon's few Democratic supporters drifted steadily away. Even staff members at the White House—a "rumor factory" in those sad days, speech writer Ray Price later called it—began maneuvering to escape blame or possible prosecution. No wonder. On July 31, John Ehrlichman was sentenced to twenty months to five years in prison for conspiracy and perjury—the fourteenth of the president's men to be convicted or to plead guilty in the complex of Watergate cases. On August 2, John Dean became the fifteenth, sent to prison for one to four years for his part in the cover-up he had later exposed. Six others, including Bob Haldeman, still faced trial on various charges.

To none of them had the president extended a helping hand—and when Haldeman asked him directly to issue a pardon for all Watergate defendants, Nixon refused (though, in his accustomed evasive manner, not to Haldeman's face). The harsh fate of so many to whom he had been close, so many who had depended on him, and some who had sacrificed for him, was bound to have moved even so reserved a man, and must have filled him with apprehension. But he offered no public contrition; instead he lapsed into frequent rages at his enemies. In later years he often claimed speciously that trying to protect his subordinates had been the cause of all his troubles; in fact, he had thrown a number of them to the wolves of the law.

Nixon tried to maintain a bold front as the summer of '74 wore on. He held meetings and made a major speech on inflation (another national concern that summer), even spent weekends at Camp David that were apparently routine (in fact, they were anything but routine). He was visited by the West German foreign minister, and during part of the summer Pat Nixon and her friend Helene Drown redecorated the Garden Room and Queen's Room in the White House.

Richard Nixon was not sleeping well, however. Often, in the middle of the night or early in the morning, he was awake and on the phone, or scribbling on one of his ubiquitous yellow legal pads. Those who saw him almost always commented on his pallor and wan appearance. Henry Kissinger, visiting San Clemente on July 26, was "shocked" at his condition and convinced that "the end of Nixon's presidency was now inevitable."

Members of a pro-Nixon group hold a vigil at the north gate of the White House, praying that Nixon not resign. August 7, 1974.

Although most of the demonstrators around the White House in those final days appeared to be calling for the president's resignation, there were others who fervently supported him.

In conversation, Nixon was more rambling than ever and, as usual, inclined to monologues. With so many of his former confidants unavailable, he spent much time with Ron Ziegler, his press secretary, and General Al Haig, who had resigned from the army to replace Haldeman as chief of staff. When Nixon conjured up one last evasive explanation of the June 23, 1972, tape, it was Haig who told him bluntly, "It's no use, Mr. President."

For nearly two years, Nixon may have suppressed memory of the tell-tale conversation with Haldeman on that fatal June day. But he had listened to a tape of it on May 6, 1974—so he had known at least since then that those incriminating words of his hung over him like the sword of Damocles. Yet, he had lied about that and other tapes even to his own attorneys, until the Supreme Court ruled against him and forced their relinquishment to Jaworski. It was only on that day, July 24, that Nixon phoned the White House from San Clemente, and in classic understatement finally told one of his lawyers, Fred Buzhardt, "There may be some problems with the June twenty-third tape, Fred."

Then, with the resignation speech to the nation on the night of August 8, it was all over, except for a rambling farewell talk to the White House staff the next day, and the departure for California of the Nixon family—still giving husband and father, despite his deceptions, their love and trust. It had been a bitter, excruciating summer, for the nation as well as the president, a wrenching time in which Richard Nixon—who had "opened" China, entered détente with Brezhnev, and won the biggest presidential victory in history—must have known that he, and only he, had brought ruin and resignation on himself. No matter how he publicly blamed enemies and denied complicity, in his deepest self and his darkest nights, he could not have escaped that hard knowledge. So, perhaps unconsciously, in that farewell talk in the White House he had sought for so many years, he spoke his own epitaph: "Always remember, others may hate you; but those who hate don't win unless you hate them—and then you destroy yourself."

Nixon was in *Air Force One,* somewhere over Missouri, when his resignation took effect and President Gerald Ford spoke his first words to the nation: "Our long national nightmare is over."

OPPOSITE
President Nixon addressing members of the cabinet and the White House staff during his farewell in the East Room of the White House on the morning of August 9, 1974. Behind Nixon are his son-in-law David Eisenhower and daughter Julie Nixon Eisenhower.

In a twenty-minute epitaph Nixon had written himself, he poured out his heart, with emotional echoes of his "Checkers" speech twenty years earlier. He attempted a determinedly upbeat delivery: "Greatness comes not when things go always good for you, but the greatness comes when you are really tested, and you take some knocks, some disappointments, when sadness comes, because only if you have been in the deepest valley can you ever know how magnificent it is to be on the highest mountain."

Gerald Warren (left), deputy press secretary, with congressmen who came to the White House to inform Nixon that they did not have the votes to prevent impeachment. Left to right: Senate Minority Leader Hugh Scott, Senator Barry Goldwater, and House Minority Leader John Rhodes at the microphone. August 7, 1974.

This visit by members of Congress was the catalytic agent that persuaded Nixon that his best option was to resign. He did not have the votes to win acquittal. It was the sad task of these men to relay that information to him. Afterward they held a press conference on the White House lawn.

Sequestered press in the Press Room of the White House on the afternoon of August 8, 1974.

To our surprise, we in the press were told on August 8 that we were to be confined to the Press Room. This was a new experience for most of us, and as time went on, people became restless. Liberties were taken that would never have been tolerated in normal times, such as newsmen driven to standing on the furniture to see what was going on outside.

The press remains sequestered in the Press Room of the White House during President Nixon's resignation speech on the evening of August 8, 1974.

The week beginning August 5, 1974, was unlike any I had ever experienced. It defined what was one of the most politically momentous events of the century. To this day I cannot remember when I sensed such dark foreboding in the White House. By the evening of August 8 we all knew we were in the final count-down and that something climactic was imminent. We, like the rest of America, had to watch television to find out what was happening just a few steps from us. Regardless of one's political persuasion, it was an emotional and sad moment that evening when President Nixon appeared on television to announce his resignation.

President Nixon
addressing members
of the cabinet and
the White House
staff during his
farewell in the
East Room of the
White House on
the morning of
August 9, 1974.

*In the final hours
of his presidency
President Nixon
bade farewell to
members of his
staff, cabinet and
friends. The band
played "Hail to
the Chief" for
the last time to
the thirty-seventh
president of the
United States.*

Helen Thomas of
UPI, listening
to President
Nixon's farewell.
August 9, 1974.

*On a national
level, this was con-
stitutional democ-
racy functioning
as it should: the
orderly, legal trans-
ference of power.
But on a human
level, I am sure no
one in the East
Room on August 9,
1974, was immune
from the intense
poignancy of
watching the
president struggle
through the emo
tional trauma of
saying "farewell."
Whether one loved
or hated Richard
Nixon, it was
almost like a death
in the family.*

OPPOSITE

Mrs. Nixon and
daughter Tricia
Nixon Cox during
President Nixon's
farewell. August 9,
1974.

*As the president
spoke, everyone
in the East Room
felt for his family,
and particularly
for Mrs. Nixon.
I remembered her
remark that the
hardest time of her
political life with
her husband had
been when he lost
his first bid for
the presidency in
November 1960.
I could not help
but feel that that
day had now been
eclipsed.*

OPPOSITE
President Nixon
addressing members
of the cabinet and
the White House staff
during his farewell.
Behind the president
is his son-in-law
David Eisenhower.

*The weeks leading
up to this traumat-
ic moment in the
life of the president
had taken a visual
toll. It took enor-
mous courage and
strength on his part
to carry off the
draining farewell
we were witnessing.
Two hours later, at
11:35 A.M., when he
was already en
route to California,
his letter of resigna-
tion was delivered
to the secretary of
state and Nixon's
presidency came
to an end.*

Henry Kissinger
with his wife, Nancy,
during President
Nixon's farewell.
August 9, 1974.

*Members of the president's administration
and their spouses filed into the East Room
for the wake of the Nixon presidency. For
them, as for the president, after months
of turmoil, the denouement was at hand.*

AFTERWORD

WATERGATE AND THE RESIGNATION OF RICHARD NIXON FROM THE PRESIDENCY changed the attitude of Americans toward their government, made presidents subject to closer scrutiny and their words more open to challenge, and sharpened the inevitable partisan rivalries between Democrats and Republicans. It established the independent prosecutor as a familiar, if not always approved, office in American government. And the fact that presidential candidates now win party nominations mostly in primaries and supposedly are financed largely by public funds can be traced, at least partially, to Richard Nixon's successful but tainted mid-Watergate campaign of 1972.

Even scandal terminology has been affected. Now every high-level controversy is likely, often without real relevance, to carry the "gate" suffix—Whitewatergate, Filegate, etc.—and every stout denial is likely to be termed "stonewalling." Victims are frequently described as "twisting slowly, slowly in the wind," a phrase John Ehrlichman memorably used in testimony before the Watergate investigating committee. And "It's not the crime that matters so much as the cover-up" has become a cliché—true enough, too, as are most clichés.

Perhaps the most consequential effect of Watergate and Nixon's resignation has been pervasive public distrust of almost any once-accepted form of authority. Together with Lyndon Johnson's "credibility gap"—the perception, sometimes correct, that Johnson was not telling the truth, at least the whole truth, about the war in Vietnam—the fate of Richard Nixon most notably diminished Americans' trust in their presidents.

When a father figure like Eisenhower, the lionized victor of World War II, was in the White House, to distrust him, except in the most narrowly partisan sense, was unthinkable. Even when the great general was caught flat-footed in the lie that the C.I.A.'s U-2 spy plane had been on a "weather mission" when it was shot down over the Soviet Union in 1960, most Americans believed that a revered president had only been trying to protect U.S. security interests. They eagerly forgave "Ike," when they noticed at all.

Nixon's stonewalling of the Watergate charges for nearly two years was an entirely different matter. Not only was he no Eisenhower, and nothing like a father figure, *his* denials of knowledge and responsibility originally concerned a common criminal case, a break-in at the Democratic National Committee headquarters, an attempted burglary quickly established to have been carried out by agents of the Committee to Re-elect the President. "I am not a crook," Nixon declared on television, and even the denial, in such words, shocked Americans.

No matter how hard the president or his associates tried, after the break-in was exposed, they could never convince enough of the public that "national security" somehow had made it necessary, much less justified. Ultimately, Nixon's own words recorded on Nixon's own tapes proved that, in an effort to obstruct justice, he had been lying to the public, to Congress, and to many of his aides. So clearly did the crucial tape expose the crime, that when one of the president's lawyers, James St. Clair, belatedly heard it, he said that he himself would become a party to obstruction of justice if the tape were not handed over to investigators.

Disclosure of that tape, at the order of the Supreme Court, brought a critical loss of support for Nixon among the Republicans—and some Democrats—who had stood by him throughout the Watergate ordeal. Only when Nixon was told to his face, with Senator Barry Goldwater taking the lead, that the Senate would convict him on the impeachment charges already voted by the House Judiciary Committee, did he finally succumb to the inevitable and resign his cherished office.

The identity of the messenger may well have had much to do with that sad decision. If Richard Nixon deserved loyalty from anyone, he deserved it from the Arizona senator whose hopeless presidential candidacy so many Republicans had crassly deserted in 1964—but for whom Dick Nixon had campaigned tirelessly to the bitter end. Goldwater was indeed loyal to the president but, honest to a fault, he was by no means a sycophant. When he, of all people, told Nixon he was through, Nixon had little choice but to believe it.

Today, a quarter-century after that confrontation forced a president's resignation, polls disclose that there has been a sharp drop in Americans' trust in politics and politicians; in local and national government; in the press, which many believe unfairly hounded Nixon; and in institutions generally. No direct connection can be proved, but pollsters seldom found such results before "Johnson's war," which Watergate so closely followed, and it seems plausible that when faith in the presidency, once the most respected of American offices, was shattered, the effect was like a spreading stain. If the president of the United States couldn't be trusted, who could be?

The damage was increased, ironically, by Gerald Ford's most controversial effort to end "our long national nightmare," his presidential pardon of Nixon. Ford had been close to Nixon all the way back to the fund crisis of 1952, when he had been among the first Republicans to telegraph his support for the beleaguered vice-presidential candidate.[1] He had been chosen by Nixon in 1974 to replace Vice President Spiro Agnew, when the latter resigned in disgrace (pleading *nolo contendere* to accepting bribes while governor of Maryland). When Ford succeeded Nixon and announced the controversial pardon for his predecessor, suspicion of a secret "deal"—the presidency for a pardon—was immediately aroused and often voiced.

Might not Ford's pardon be a prearranged *quid pro quo* for the resignation that had made him president? No substantial evidence ever has been adduced to sustain this suspicion, and Ford—whose reputation for probity has largely withstood the charge—insists that he considered the pardon necessary to avoid any possibility that a former president might be put on trial for criminal charges. But the suspicion persists and almost certainly was instrumental in Ford's narrow defeat by Jimmy Carter in 1976—the only Democratic presidential victory in the twenty-four years and five presidential campaigns between Richard Nixon's first election and that of Bill Clinton in 1992.

Since Watergate and Nixon's resignation, moreover, the public's attitude toward politicians' tactics also has changed for the worse. American politics "ain't beanbag," as one early practitioner put it, and never has been pure. But the tactics of the C.R.P. in 1972 came to be widely considered unacceptably "dirty"—or shady politics, at the least. At about the same time, television became the major instrument of campaigning (especially in large constituencies). It permits misstatements, overstatements, high- and low-road tactics to have greater impact on a wider audience than ever; and as politicians have long known, denial and rebuttal seldom catch up even with an unsupported charge. "Negative" campaigning—imputing evil or venality to an opponent, sometimes in lieu of proving one's own virtue—has been spurred by television. Combined with near-legendary tales about the C.R.P.'s "dirty tricks" and its rank financial dealings in 1972, this has lent an aura of duplicity and lack of scruple to all political campaigning. Over the years, further offenses, alleged or proven, have only emphasized the prevailing idea that politics is "dirty."

The uninhibited fundraising of the C.R.P. and other Nixon associates led also to the establishment of the Federal Elections Commission and to limited public financing of presidential campaigns. After that, availability of public funds allowed lesser-known persons to seek the presidency, which in turn led to the greater influence of state primary elections, in which, ostensibly, candidates can prove their vote-getting abilities. Today, winning primaries is far more important than having influential connections in achieving a party nomination, so the system of choosing presidential nominees also has been revolutionized since 1972—the last year of the so-called "old politics" in which Richard Nixon flourished.

This change also was sped along by reforms within the Democratic party, aimed at rectifying the process by which, in 1968, Hubert Humphrey's nomination had been forced by Lyndon Johnson and other party leaders, although Eugene McCarthy and Robert Kennedy had won most of the primaries. Humphrey had entered *no* primaries. After 1972, the Democrats made another such victory impossible and participation in primaries all but mandatory; the Republicans soon were forced to follow.

The Watergate charges were investigated by two independent prosecutors; Congress had established their office in the belief that an attorney general appointed by a president could not necessarily be trusted to investigate that president, if it became necessary. So Archibald Cox, a Harvard professor, was first appointed; he was fired by Nixon in the celebrated Saturday Night Massacre, during which Attorney General Elliot Richardson also resigned in protest. Leon Jaworski, a renowned Texas attorney, then was appointed and served until the end of the investigation and Nixon's resignation.

Numerous "independent" (of the administration in power) prosecutors have served since then, under varying rules of procedure and with varying results, notably during the administrations of Ronald Reagan and Bill Clinton. The performance of "independent" prosecutor Kenneth Starr in the inquiry into Clinton's pre-presidential financial activities (Whitewatergate) and sexual adventures (Monicagate) was so controversial, and many believed so partisan, that the propriety of the office itself, particularly the power of an investigator to act outside of either presidential or congressional check, repeatedly was called into question by legal authorities and political leaders. It was considered unlikely that the legislation authorizing such "independent" prosecutors would be renewed as hearings on the question began in 1999.

Another fallout from Nixon's resignation was highly visible more than twenty years later—the investigation of Clinton and his impeachment. There is no doubt today about Richard Nixon's specific guilt in obstructing justice; his own tapes amply proved the case. But bitter questions linger in many minds as to whether he should, as a result, have been impeached or forced to resign. Head counts at the time supported Barry Goldwater's blunt judgment—had the impeachment charges gone to trial in the Senate in 1974, Nixon almost surely would have been convicted and removed from office. But did the offenses alleged really rise to the level of the "high crimes and misdemeanors" the Constitution specifies as grounds for impeachment and removal? Or was it not actually the case that the long-despised "Tricky Dick" was a victim of Democratic partisanship, Democratic power in Congress in 1974, and the virulent dislike of the "liberal press"? Many still believe that was so.

Bill Clinton's guilt on another specific charge—lying to the public, to colleagues, and to congressional Democrats about a sexual liaison with a White House intern—was as clear as Nixon's offense became in 1974. Clinton finally admitted the affair and the lie and begged the public's pardon. Again, however, as the case unfolded, it was not uncommon to hear mostly Democrats assert that, whatever the president's misdeeds or admissions, Clinton, too, was a victim—this time of a partisan prosecutor and a thirst for revenge by Republicans who had never forgiven or forgotten Nixon's ouster and never reconciled themselves to a Democratic president[2]—particularly the "draft dodger" Bill Clinton. And unlike 1974, Republicans controlled Congress in 1998 with a majority in the House sufficient to vote an impeachment.

Republicans still controlled the House and the Senate in 1999, but again the old question arose: did the charges against Clinton—sex in the White House and its cover-up—constitute the Constitutionally-specified high crimes or misdemeanors? And since Clinton's obstruction of justice, if any, came in a private matter rather than on official presidential business, it often was asserted that Republicans and conservatives, with the help of Prosecutor Starr and with echoes of Watergate ringing in their ears, were mainly out to get Clinton. The supposed weakness of the case as well as the aura of vengeance in which it was considered were primary among reasons why even in a Republican Senate, Clinton was acquitted on the impeachment charges.

The question was somewhat different during the Reagan administration in the "Iran-Contra" scandal (known, naturally, as "Irangate"). In the Reagan case, the president himself frequently had proclaimed that he would never exchange arms for hostages, such as those Americans held by Iran during the Carter administration, or reward terrorists with American arms. In his second term, startlingly, it was disclosed that officers of his administration had, in fact, sold arms to Iran and then used the proceeds to subsidize the anti-Communist Contras in Nicaragua—a force Congress had specifically refused to finance. Had Reagan known? Or had an elderly president been sufficiently inattentive to his duty to permit his subordinates to act illegally without his knowledge?

Again, as in Watergate, there were loud Democratic and liberal cries for impeachment—as in 1999 there were Republican demands for Clinton's head. But in a series of televised Senate hearings and later public trials, Reagan subordinates assumed responsibility and absolved the president himself from guilty knowledge or dereliction of duty, claiming righteously that they were only acting in a national interest thwarted by an anti-Reagan Democratic Congress.

Reagan's original predicament had been serious enough that Arthur Liman, the staff chief of the Senate investigating committee, predicted the president would have to resign.[3] But so much blame was shifted from Reagan by aides and so adroitly did the president avoid the fatal appearance of engaging in a cover-up that he survived—though he was widely considered to have been inattentive or gullible, or both. Some students of the case believe to this day that Reagan *did* know that arms were being exchanged for hostages and that the Contras were being illicitly funded. If so, he could have been impeached for deceiving the public and for ignoring the expressed will of Congress.

Except in the echoes of Richard Nixon's resignation, however, the question of removing a popular president from office—either Reagan or Clinton—might never have arisen. The last impeachment before that threatened against Nixon was of President Andrew Johnson after the Civil War, and he was acquitted in the Senate (by a single vote). In the intervening century, until the case of Richard Nixon, impeaching a president and removing him from office never had been a real or practical likelihood.

Now, as those who have followed the Clinton inquiry know, impeachment proceedings have a recent precedent, perhaps a partisan motive, a possible instrument in the "independent prosecutor," and therefore can no longer be considered a mere Constitutional abstraction. The removal of a president—Richard Nixon—has been accomplished once and within memory. So it could and might be done again. That possibility is bound to have changed, however subliminally, the attitude of an American public not, in any case, as certain of its values as it once was. Among other doubts, Americans now know their presidents can misbehave and lie about it. He, perhaps someday she, is no longer a fact fixed in the firmament for four and probably eight years. Now the president—at least in public perception—may be as impermanent as a member of Congress, or a mayor, and is little more to be relied upon. And that may be the final judgment on Richard Nixon—that he weakened the great office he had sought for so long, and had sworn to uphold.

As for Nixon the man, even in his involuntary retirement he retained much of his dignity and his accustomed manner. In an unusual display of emotion for so reserved a person, he did confess to David Frost in a television interview, while fighting back tears, that he had "let down my friends . . . let down the country. . . . Let down the American people."

After his resignation, however, he wasted no time vacating the White House and returning to California. He maintained a mostly stoic demeanor, and in his best comeback style bested a potentially fatal attack of phlebitis. Then, with his fabled tenacity, he set himself on the road to rehabilitation.

Moving first to New York, then to New Jersey, he never sought public office again but maintained a keen interest in politics and a subtle hand in Republican affairs. Publishing numerous books on leaders he had known and on matters of policy, as well as *RN,* he became probably the best—certainly the most prolific—presidential writer since Theodore Roosevelt. In occasional public appearances and speeches, as well as blameless personal behavior, he even reestablished himself as a respected commentator, a "wise old head," particularly on international affairs.

When Nixon died in 1994, obituaries dwelled, of course, on the singular fact of his life— that he was the first, and so far the only, president forced to resign under threat of conviction on impeachment charges. Once again, other significant achievements of his life and his presidency, and there were many, had to take a secondary place. Nevertheless, at his funeral in California, members of the party he had served so long recognized him in death as few had been willing to do in the last years of his life. Thousands of the American people, moreover, stood in mile-long lines to honor him again, as they had in twice electing him president, and in giving him about as much of their favor and as many of their votes as they had given John Kennedy in 1960.

The funeral took place only a few miles from Whittier, where in his youth Richard Nixon had risen before so many dawns to work in the family grocery. That was far from a true measure of the distance he had traveled, or of the difficulty of his journey.

1. Another was Warren Burger, whom Nixon later nominated to be chief justice of the Supreme Court.
2. Revenge also, some assert, for a Democratic Senate's refusal to confirm Ronald Reagan's nomination of Robert Bork for the Supreme Court.
3. In a private conversation with a columnist of the *New York Times*.